Organisationskommunikation |
Organisational Communication

herausgegeben von / edited by

Mag. Dr. Thomas Duschlbauer MA,
Fachhochschule St. Pölten

FH.-Prof. Mag. (FH) Dr. Johanna Grüblbauer,
Fachhochschule St. Pölten

Mag.ª Dr.in Sieglinde Martin, FHWien der WKW

FH.-Prof. Mag. Dr. Peter Winkler, FHWien der WKW

Band / Volume 5

Thomas Duschlbauer

Performative Change

Digitisation and the Organisational Turn
from Dogma to Style

Nomos
Edition Reinhard Fischer

The Deutsche Nationalbibliothek lists this publication in the
Deutsche Nationalbibliografie; detailed bibliographic data
are available on the Internet at http://dnb.d-nb.de

ISBN   978-3-8487-5128-0 (Print)
          978-3-8452-9329-5 (ePDF)

British Library Cataloguing-in-Publication Data
A catalogue record for this book is available from the British Library.

ISBN   978-3-8487-5128-0 (Print)
          978-3-8452-9329-5 (ePDF)

Library of Congress Cataloging-in-Publication Data
Duschlbauer, Thomas
Performative Change
Digitisation and the Organisational Turn from Dogma to Style
Thomas Duschlbauer
125 pp.
Includes bibliographic references.

ISBN   978-3-8487-5128-0 (Print)
          978-3-8452-9329-5 (ePDF)

Onlineversion
Nomos eLibrary

1st Edition 2020
© Nomos Verlagsgesellschaft, Baden-Baden, Germany 2020. Printed and bound in
Germany.

Acknowledgements

I would like to take this opportunity to thank my colleague FH-Prof. Johanna Grüblbauer for her comments as well as the students at the universities where I have taught over the past years—especially those students from Johannes Kepler University from the web innovation course, who have been very open to exciting discussions.

Table of Contents

Preface

While Donald Trump announced at a press conference in the White House Rose Garden that he was mobilising the military against so-called "lawless" and rioting people to protect peaceful protesters, at the same time and almost in the same place, the brutal violence of the authorities was felt by the very same people. This was an irritating moment, probably unparalleled in history—as was Trump's subsequent appearance for the press holding a Bible in his hands in front of a church barricaded with planks.

The linguist John Langshaw Austin calls such forms of articulation performative acts, especially since they not only represent and verbally describe reality, but also change it (1). Trump's speech in front of journalists in the Rose Garden is directly linked to action, which is why one can speak of it as a political event, just as when a tunnel is opened by cutting a ribbon or a minister is sworn in on the Bible.

This performativity also simultaneously represents a contrast or antipole to the creation of what we today call "alternative facts": While in the performative act speaking and acting form a unity and thus the spoken word communicates something together with physical movements, the communication of alternative facts refers to events that may or may not have taken place in another form. Actual facts, in the sense of being something "true", do not necessarily have to be performative acts—for example, if an illusionist uses a magic spell to make a rabbit disappear before our eyes during his/her show, then we can also assume that the rabbit has not really vanished into thin air.

This "disappearance" is then simply something illusory and, strictly speaking, a question of interpretation. The rabbit has only "disappeared" because we suddenly no longer see it, which does not mean that it could not actually be somewhere else. Even in the case of the dissolution of the demonstrations in front of the White House, it is a question of interpretation whether the people gathered were peaceful citizens or, in the eyes of Trump, a violent mob.

Because of the significance of interpretation, the performative act is not only dependent on the staging but also the authority of the person acting. For example, many people recognise more truth in what is factual if the protagonists wear a white coat, are proficient in Latin or are recommended by other important personalities. In this respect, the discussion about performativity is also impossible to separate from aspects such as power and, ultimately, knowledge. This is also because, conversely, authority can also be derived directly from performative acts—as in the case of Boris Yeltsin, for example, who in August 1991, after the thwarted coup, deprived Michael Gorbachev of his power in front of running cameras by signing a decree, thus sealing the further fate of the then Soviet Union and Communist Party.

Against this background, performative acts and the creation of alternative facts are structurally opposed, but from the perspective of power, they are something that maintains and can further strengthen it through certain combinatorics. For example, the inauguration of a president is apparently not in itself sufficient to convey the desired authority—in comparison to his predecessor—which is why those responsible for public relations invent a few thousand more people to be present at this event. Conversely, however, alternative facts seem more credible to us if they are disseminated by people with high authority. In this respect, both activities support each other in order to increase the effectiveness of the actors through their language and their images in public.

This applies not only to politics, but also to business organisations. Perhaps it is therefore not surprising if, for example, in the case of a company like Wirecard on a platform for employer evaluations, the first of these evaluations is titled "It's all about appearances". Although Wirecard also had the typical nimbus of a modern tech company, its collapse has now shown that an extremely rigid and ritualised corporate culture was at work there, with a strictly hierarchical system, esprit de corps and oaths of loyalty to the management board (2). This is certainly an extreme and not necessarily a representative example, especially since in creating alternative facts vis-à-vis investors and controlling authorities, criminal energies were probably also released. However, it shows to what extent even in companies the entanglement of performative acts and alternative facts can lead to an organisation losing more and more groundedness and reference to reality. This example also shows that free drinks, the weekly fruit basket and the subscription to the gym do not necessarily have anything to do with New Work or an agile organisation—especially if an organisation switches to animation mode due to a lack of orientation.

This is exactly where the term "performativity" can be located in many corporate organisations. While the performative could actually serve as an emancipatory and participatory instrument of change—as long as this has not long since been established as an end in itself—the ideas of those in charge are still dominated by the image of a stage, which on the one hand maintains the separation between actors and audience and on the other hand functions as a vehicle to spread, garnished with elements of story-telling and amusing anecdotes, what should give employees a pleasant gut feeling in order to strengthen identification, cooperation and motivation. So it's still all about worshipping consensus as a golden calf and pulling out all kinds of staged stops for it.

The concept of performativity, however, prefers the contradictory and also recognises deviations in the sequence of imitations, counter-imitations, quotations, etc. in social practices. Indeed, it even goes so far as not even to assume the existence of the original as such, which is why it is critical of the cult of genius and commercially exploitable founder myths. None of this actually fits into an economic environment, where almost only disruption is required rather than change in small and barely noticeable steps.

At the same time, everyone knows that they are actually subject to a promise that is only fulfilled for a few; a promise that on the one hand puts employees in a constant state of alarm and exhausts them, and that also costs management a great deal of energy in keeping up appearances to the outside world with its customers and other stakeholders.

The "outside" is now also endeavouring to adapt to the mechanisms of corporate marketing with its performative actionism. While there was talk of greenwashing in the past, Mercedes is apparently throwing itself into expenses and painting its Formula 1 racing cars black. And Facebook users are also have done this with great enthusiasm with their profile pictures, thus adding to the list of actions that certainly follow a well-meant intention but are, in principle, empty and meaningless gestures.

The social human being, like the somnabule, is caught in the illusion of holding ideas that are suggested to them as spontaneous inventions of themselves. But it is precisely at the somnabule that the imitative passivity of the social being becomes apparent (3), as we experience it in social networks, where it is sufficient to like things and simply to share them. Insofar, for those slacktivists it is much easier to express sympathy or to point their fingers at others in the sense of shaming them than to really act and make sacrifices yourself. And it is also much easier to destroy or remove anything where we are confronted with ambivalence or irony and therefore have to use our intellect and possibly expose ourselves to tiresome discussions with people who resist consensus. Finally, these discursive or respectively non-discursive practices are also increasingly tending towards dogma, fanaticism and self-righteousness.

The creation of a reality in a performative sense does not require the simultaneous extinction of other possibilities. It is no longer just a matter of ideals such as enlightenment and education, but of the special competence to endure other and possibly contradicting constructions of the world.

The speech of Donald Trump as speech act.

Image 1: Thomas Duschlbauer

References:

(1) Austin, John Longshaw (1972). Zur Theorie der Sprechakte (How to do things with Words). Deutsche Bearbeitung von Eike von Savigny. Stuttgart, Reclam

(2) Neuscheler, Tillmann & Peitsmeier, Henning (2020). Der Fall Wirecard: Mit Korpsgeist und Treueschwüren. In: FAZ 22.07.2020. link: 07.24.2020: https://www.faz.net/aktuell/wirtschaft/wirecard-mit-korpsgeist-und-treueschwueren-16872208.html

(3) Baier, Karl (2013). Somnabulismus als Medium der Vergesellschaftung. Mesmerisch beeinflusste Auffassungen des Sozialen vom 18. zum späten 19. Jahrhundert. In: Nacim Ghanbari & Marcus Hahn (Hrsg.). Reinigungsarbeit. transcript, Zeitschrift für Kulturwissenschaften, Heft 1/2013, p. 78

Introduction

"It is time that organisation theory became fully aware of its pedigree. It is time for it to think more consciously about the social philosophy on which it is based. In short, it is time that it became more fully aware of its relationship to the 'big issues'. Only by grounding itself in a knowledge of its past and of the alternative avenues for development can it realise its full potential in the years ahead."
Gibson Burrell/ Gareth Morgan (1)

Digitisation not only produces a plenitude of applications that we could use in a working environment. It also phenomenologically calls into question the very nature of labour, organisation and communication, and in the context of digitisation we should by no means refrain from dealing with this change at an overarching level.

With the widespread use of the 5G standard at the latest, digital uses are possible that, together with other digital applications, also affect fundamental aspects of our existence in the world. Given the scale of digitisation, the debate is likely to be short-lived if it remains within the framework of user centricity and there is no holistic analysis of what also affects the changes in the human condition.

Marshall McLuhan, for example, pointed out in 1958, long before the advent of digitisation and the development of the Internet, that the media also functions as a message (2). In this respect, the selection of the media used does not only concern the form of "presentation" and "preparation" of content but is itself a content that influences our perception of our image of the world and our interaction. Even if the Internet in itself only allows connections and does not represent any content on its own, it can still be a trigger for narratives.

There is also the fact that the application of technology itself can be perceived as an event or a sensation. For example, Mood Design consciously focuses on staging technology in everyday life in such a way that special experiences are evoked in the users and certain feelings are triggered. For some millenials, the first contact with an iPhone was probably just as formative as the memory of the first moon landing was for the earliest representatives of Generation X.

For an enthusiastic car driver, on the other hand, it is a special attraction when the start-stop button of the vehicle flickers red in the rhythm of a heartbeat before it is pressed. This technical analogy to a natural process in our body represents emotionalising aspects such as tension, strength and vitality. Thus, technology is able to penetrate all areas of our everyday life and to contribute to the fact that our lives are increasingly subjected to stagings that surprise us, intensify feelings and distract us from routine. However, technology in these examples is always fed back to our skills and abilities, because the purpose of such stagings is to establish a reference to our traits and personality by showing that we are operating (bedienen) and mastering (beherrschen) technology. In this constellation, we assume the role of a master and servant, and those who cannot serve cannot rule. Personal sovereignty in our technological world is also derived from the skills with which we face new technical challenges.

In the sense of Sigmund Freud's cultural theory, Arnold Gehlen's anthropology and sociology or McLuhan's media theory, our technologies make us "prosthetic gods" (3), "deficient beings" (Mängelwesen) (4) or beings who use media as extensions of their sense organs (5). Until recently, technology always appeared as a compensation for human deficits or as an amplification of existing abilities. Their use required a physical and mental aptitude from the human being, which continued to suggest a certain superiority.

From this compensatory and amplifying relationship between humankind and its technologies, sports disciplines, for example, were derived. In the handling of technical devices such as airplanes or automobiles, it is no longer capabilities such as strength and endurance that count, but sensory talents such as a quick reaction or a good perception of how a machine behaves when exposed to extreme physical forces. It is these phenomena, for example, that contribute so much to the fascination of motor sports. The unity of man and machine results precisely from the fact that the deficits of one are compensated by the strengths of the other.

Future technologies, however, will ensure that we share our world with robots, mutants, androids, avatars and other new "beings" and that we interact and communicate with them. The spheres of the purely material and the organic are increasingly networked and interwoven, digital technology is implanted within the organism, while we live with our bodies in the smart homes of the smart cities and while we are transported from A to B by smart mobility.

Smart does not necessarily mean what we may associate with "intelligent". Smart is not necessarily clever or even wise but has something to do with dexterity and capability. Being smart doesn't just mean thinking, it's a way of thinking that's very closely connected to doing. After all, digital technology is also there to do something for us humans or for what will remain of our human existence. This connection of a special characteristic of the ability to think with doing can best be described as a skill, whereby the skill as "readiness" also has something fatelike in it and thus also points to an irrevocable order – similar to the etymology of the term "data" which also points to something already "given".

If, in this new order, things confront us autonomously with their peculiar dexterity in order to relieve us of all the burdens of our existence, then the question naturally arises as to whether human dexterity does not at some point wither away to the mere and ultimately no longer expressed talent? In a direct sense, we would no longer be effective, because it is no longer we who operate the machines, but we are operated all around by the machines. For example, we sit in a self-propelled motor vehicle and are driven without directly experiencing the forces that we still trigger and tame ourselves through our actions today. We move around and no longer have direct contact with the physical forces acting on us. We don't even have to look out of the window while driving, because we can blindly trust the technology working in the background.

While the automotive industry has been giving us the serum of an exciting and refreshing driving experience for decades in order to sell its highly emotionalised products, there is hardly any difference between a self-propelled car and other things of everyday life such as office furniture or refrigerators. Like freight, we are sent from A to B by the car without having to show any dexterity. Driving a car is more or less a logistical process, comparable to a sexual act that is functionally oriented exclusively towards reproduction.

What happens to us from an ontological perspective when we are confronted with a different scope of action through an autonomously deciding and acting technology and are therefore confronted with a different fullness and quality of experience? What about our potential to act if, in Spinoza's sense, the human body is now possibly excited or affected in a different way or even less? For Spinoza, there is a close connection between man's ability to act and his ability to become affected, whereby the ability to act is an expression of the human being and at the same time the affirmation of what we consider to be the ability to be impressed and influenced (6).

Moreover, an autonomous digital technology is not oriented towards an environment of ambiguity and diversity, which would make it difficult for the machine to make decisions for us. The development of artificial intelligence has little sense of humour and even less of irony. What is generally considered an entertainment factor for us humans – at least for the more intelligent among us – is ultimately based on decisions. Because irony offers at least two versions of a possible reality and we feel something like pleasure in weighing, testing, deciding and learning from an ambivalent situation. So far, social change has always been shaped and driven by such learning experiences out of ambivalent situations, and in Romanticism irony even became a self-reflexive stylistic device, an aesthetic theory.

So far, for the first time in the history of humankind, technology does not appear in its classical compensatory and amplifying, but in an autonomous manner. And the changes that are brought about by it will increasingly no longer be processed through the path of ambiguity and diversity and, for example, the resulting irony. For the task of the machine now is precisely to take decisions from us in all areas of everyday life, which is why ambiguity is nothing more than an inadequacy (7). Besides the Conditio humana, there is now a Conditio technica too, a technical being, which aims at simply reading human needs and deciding for us.

Technology serves man and man serves technology by shaping the world for it in such a way that it becomes increasingly unambiguous, thus paving the way for machines to take on this certain form of symbiotic care.

The philosopher Éric Sadin draws the conclusion from this that humankind is repositioned in two ways: On the one hand in an otological respect, since it is no longer the only being endowed with the ability to judge and is displaced by the new instance of truth, which humankind itself regards as superior. On the other hand, we would be anthropologically marginalised, since it is no longer the human being who exercises creative power with the help of his mind, his senses and his knowledge, but rather a power of interpretation and decision regarded as more capable. According to Sadin, this would displace humankind from different life worlds, beginning with the world of labour (8).

While at the beginning of the information age the concept of information was still predominantly linked with the meaning of notifying and teaching, this is now changing and the second and original meaning of this concept, or the Latin form, is coming to the fore. The world of things is adapted to the requirements of the digital world, so that things no longer have to be laboriously identified in a chaos but can be recognised at any time and in any place. The concept of information in the sense of an autonomously occurring technology operated by black-box-like algorithms is necessarily also about forming and imprinting in a material or phenotypic sense. For this, technology in its function no longer refers solely to humankind as a deficient being, but also to nature. If its evolution is a permanent process of adaptation, then it also reveals defects, which can even be remedied, for example, by correcting the environmental conditions in such a way that nature no longer has to adapt to conditions such as those envisaged by the utopia of terraforming on distant planets by robots and other machines.

Information is therefore no longer merely a process of perception and imagination in animals and humans, as Augustine analyses in his Platon-influenced treatise "On the Trinity". It is no longer just a matter of sensual looking as a process in which the object informs the sensory perception (informatio senus) (9). No, as the ideas of the Internet of Things or of industry 4.0, for example, reveal, for the first time it is also about objects and their spatial-temporal arrangement.

However, the sphere of the informative, which is now equipped with a new authority to act towards the formative, is also confronted with the sphere of the performative. It could now help humankind to regain for itself the very function of information that had receded into the background in the course of the digitalisation and autonomisation of technology. Together with other people, human beings can form their own image of their self in their virtues, talents and abilities through the performative. In humankinds remaining niche with its remaining scope for action, it can try itself out in the performative and educate itself.

According to John Longshaw Austin's philosophical approach to language, there is also a distinction between constative and performative utterances. While the constative utterances, which also correspond to the binary logic of the digital sphere, follow a true false classification, the performative articulation, which is action-related in the sense of "doing something" and puts something into effect (10), contrasts with this. The performative, with its reality-generating and material character, could, precisely in times of this fundamental change, create a balance to the effectiveness of the digital and contribute to social innovation being able to keep up with that of our technologies. Shannon Jackson also points out that performance has two dimensions: One that refers to collaboration, which represents the conditions and content of performance – and one that, in its various forms, creates the possibility of re-establishing community (11).

Performance or the staging, the game, the masquerade or the spectacle is thus to be seen not merely as entertainment or part of the event industry, but as an emancipatory method in which no analyses are prescribed before action is taken, but rather immediate analyses of action, experimentation and improvisation, from which the scope of action of an individual or a group can also be derived. In order to regain, maintain, or further develop skills via the path of doing, it is therefore a matter of a theory of performativity as a critical theory of action in the age of digital practices. It seems useful to include post-dramatic theatrical discourses and to trace the development from the "lingustic turn" to the "performative turn" in general.

This method can be to some extend considered as related to iterative approaches such as Design Thinking or Bricolage, because all of these approaches build on a creative and transformational understanding of learning and inquiry. They mark a shift from a belief mode, focused on the plausibility and justification of ideas, towards a design mode, which is oriented towards the utility and "promissingness" of ideas. Rather than solely focusing on what already exists, they aim to examine what might be, to explore systems and states that do not yet exist. Such design methods are, to a large extent, nowadays focused on new products, services and business models, and are aimed at finding innovative solutions. This performative approach intends to be able to transform an organisation and to empower its stakeholders not only to react to new realities, but also to create their own reality.

If we consequently follow this path from simple "Design Thinking" over "Design from Within" to "Design as Inquiry" (12) and rethink it radically, the relationship between the means and the purpose – that is, between production and the product and between creation and the artefact – also is reversed. Seen in this manner, it is not necessarily the organisation and socialisation of human beings that enables them to create artifacts, but rather the artifact or respectively the process of its creation may serve to bring people together, to enable them to acquire new competences, to cultivate virtues, to identify with others – and ultimately to create organisation at a higher level in order to face new challenges.

So, this is not just a purely academic consideration, but essentially depends on how we define ourselves as people, what we identify with and from what source we derive the motivation for our existence. This is all the more true as the automation of processes – e.g. via algorithms and bots etc. – is increasingly regarded as desirable both at the level of communication and at the level of the organisation.

References:
1. Burrell, Gibson & Morgan, Gareth (1979). Sociological Paradigms and Organisational Analysis. London/ Exeter, NH. Heinemann
2. McLuhan mentioned this for the first time in 1958 during a lecture (vgl. Marchand 1998, S. 198). Later in: McLuhan, Marshall (1964). Understanding Media. London, Routledge & Kegan, p. 29
3. Freud, Sigmund (1974). Das Unbehagen in der Kultur. In: Sigmund Freud: Studienausgabe, Bd. 9. Frankfurt a. M., S. Fischer, p. 222
4. Gehlen, Arnold (2016). Der Mensch. Seine Natur und seine Stellung in der Welt. Frankfurt a. M., Klostermann, pp. 35 – 36
5. McLuhan, Marshall (1964). p. 68
6. Müller, Gin (2015). Possen des Performativen. Wien, Transversal, pp. 52 – 53
7. Bauer, Thomas (2018). Die Vereindeutigung der Welt. Über den Verlust an Mehrdeutigkeit und Vielfalt. Stuttgart, Reclam, p. 92
8. Sadin, Éric (7. Juni 2017). Das geht zu weit! In: Die Zeit, Nr. 24, p. 8
9. Augustinus, Aurelius (2002). On the Trinity. Cambridge, Cambridge University Press, trin. 11,2,3
10. Austin, John. L. (1986). Performative Äußerungen. In: Ders. Gesammelte philosophische Aufsätze. Stuttgart, Reclam, pp. 305 – 327
11. Jackson, Shannon (2011). Social Worlds. Performing Art, Supporting Publics. London/New York: Routledge, pp. 11 – 17
12. Allert, Heidrun & Richter, Christoph (2009). Design as Open-Ended Inquiry. In: V. Hornung-Prähauser, M. Luckmann and D. Wieden-Bischof (Ed.). Creativity and Innovation Competencies on the Web. 5th Interdisciplinary EduMedia Conference, Salzburg, Austria, May 4-5, 2008. Salzburg Research

* Parts of the introduction were also published by Springer Verlag in the conference proceedings of the 11th Scientific Conference on Event Research (Events und Messen im digitalen Zeitalter) under the title "Digitaler Wandel und Performativität" (pp. 156 – 174)

From transcendence to immanence

One of the central topoi of postmodern theory was the idea that consciousness leaves its system of biological brain, nervous electrics and physical integration in order to expose itself to other system combinations – apparative hardware and "symbolic" software – and that this emigration is not simply about outsourcing or respectively the expansion of our consciousness, but about a complete new system – with an implicit, exclusively own, irreducible "logic" of technisation (1).

Of course, technology also played a central role during the modern era before. Insofar, this age was marked by the belief in progress and also by the conviction that even problems caused by technologies can be solved with new and superior technologies. Moreover, we must not forget that the foundations of the technologies that are now driving digitisation are based on reflections, discoveries and inventions made in modern and pre-modern times.

In this respect, for example, the topoi of human immortality through the use of technology is not that new as well as the scientific analysis of the human brain, to which it is attributed that it is able to construct reality. However, it is precisely this complex organ that can be used as an example to show how much science as such is influenced by the construction of reality too. This example is also worth mentioning because the brain is not only a model for research on artificial intelligence but is also frequently used as a metaphor for a learning organisation. A central question in these approaches concerning this metaphor is whether organisations can be designed in such a way that they can learn and organise themselves like a fully functioning brain. Apart from the fact that this metaphor takes no account whatsoever of existing power structures within an organisation, it is also questionable whether at the present time we actually relate our ideas of a learning organisation to what is happening in our brains.

In 1817 Mary Shelley published her novel "Frankenstein or: The modern Prometheus". In it, the legendary monster is brought to life by the ingenious physician Dr. Viktor Frankenstein using an early form of electrotherapy. This book, which she wrote at the age of 17, was obviously inspired by the experiments of the physician Luigi Galvani, who in his experiments with electricity came to the conclusion that electricity would also play an important role for processes in our body (2).

About 200 years after the publication of this novel, if the will of the physician Sergio Canavero is to be fulfilled, then mankind will soon be transplanting a head onto the body of another human being for the first time. This operation, which is highly controversial among experts, is supposed to take place in China, for which a team of around 100 specialists has already been formed (3).

Without the possibilities of digitisation, this already daring undertaking would be doomed to failure from the outset. For example, it would be just as impossible to find a suitable brain-dead donor as it would be to accustom the patient to his/her new body, which is to be made easier by means of virtual reality. No one can predict the success of such a project, but it is already clear that digitisation will ultimately be far more than the mere use of technology to make our everyday lives easier. The effects of this development will ultimately help us to redefine ourselves as people and in our relationship to things. Because this change is not only about shaping the world differently with our thinking, but these new technologies will also cause us to submit thinking itself to a completely new reflection. Not only what we think about, but especially how we think and which kinds of thinking we can possibly even outsource to machines will gain importance in the future (4).

Of course, we can also look at digitisation from a completely different perspective and claim that it is actually an old hat: computers have been around since the 1950s. The basic technologies for the internet already existed in the 1970s, and pioneers like Jaron Lanier and Marvin Minsky made terms like virtual reality and artificial intelligence popular for the first time in the 1980s. At the latest the time thereafter is attributed to the fifth Kontratieff cycle as a transition from the industrial to the information society, which we today call the knowledge society. The key technology fact is, however, that digitalisation has now reached such a level of maturity as a result of this prehistory that it is relatively easy to integrate this technology into every conceivable area of life. Not only that, but it also makes it possible for more and more people to participate in or control processes from which they were previously excluded due to a lack of technical prerequisites or high costs. Examples of this are miniaturisation, which is expressed in 3D printers among other things, or the open source movement. Even the so-called sharing culture could not function without digital participation in the organisation.

This makes many things easier and more accessible, but also gives rise to certain risks and the extent of which cannot yet be assessed today. For example, the media and the sciences are associated with the fact that their authority over information and interpretation is currently being massively questioned. It has therefore become even more difficult to pursue an objective discourse on the meaningful and ethically justifiable use of the new technical achievements, particularly as a result of the possibilities offered by digitisation – like bots and the simplicity with which messages can be manipulated on a grand scale today.

These innovations are also backed by powerful economic interests. One example of this is artificial intelligence, in whose research billions are invested worldwide every year and which is also closely linked to the findings of neuroscience. Since the beginnings of the computer in the 1940s and 1950s until today, the view has prevailed that our brain also works like a computer.

It is interesting to note that in the history of science there has obviously always been a connection between the supposed function of the brain and current scientific innovations. For example, René Descartes, best known for his methodological doubt, which he resolved with the sentence "I think, therefore I am", was also one of the first neurophysiologists and, after many years of research, came to the conclusion in 1637 that animals were mere automatons (5). Thinkers like him or Hobbes, inspired by the first automatons, assumed that our brain would be controlled by tiny mechanical movements. Later, when there were notable discoveries about chemistry and electricity in the 18th century, the metaphors for our thinking changed accordingly as we can see it at Mary Shelley's "Frankenstein" and similar novells and news stories of this time.

From the 19th century onwards, the achievements in the field of communication were added, culminating in the German physicist Hermann von Helmholtz assuming that the brain would function like a telegraph (6). No wonder, then, that the mathematician John von Neumann, for example, simply stated in his book "The Computer and the Brain" in 1958 that the brain functions like a digital calculator (7). Conversely, neuroscientists are not so sure. And they can't be, because they know that they are dealing with an extremely complex object and that their basic research is only just beginning.

Today, they can only attest that our brain can store information, but how and where this information is stored in the cells is a matter of speculation. The latest findings also point in the direction that it is less important how the neurons exchange information with each other than what happens inside the cells. And now we are experiencing that the state of knowledge is once again moving in exactly the same direction as the scientific discipline, which is currently making very new discoveries like quantum physics. Since 1996, for example, the physicists Stuart Hameroff and Sir Roger Penrose have been working on the quantum theory of consciousness. They assume that the soul sits in tiny vessels in the brain cells. Our brain would therefore not only possess an immortal consciousness and not just work like an ordinary computer, but function more like a quantum computer (8). So, what now? Back again to Descartes in the 17th century? With his dualism he also tried to prove that mind and matter were two different "substances".

In the 20th century, also the philosopher Sir Karl Popper as well as the Nobel laureate and neurophysiologist John Eccles had the opinion that there must be interaction between the brain and the consciousness and that our I could exist without a brain (9). It cannot therefore be ruled out that enormous sums will be invested in research projects which maybe are based on questionable premises.

It may also be questionable whether in such circumstances we should strive for a transhumanism that expands the limits of our intellectual, physical and psychological possibilities through technology and also protects us from the possible negative effects of an artificial and possibly even superior intelligence. The hope for salvation and transcendence after death, which has always been articulated by humans, now leads to the expectation of the optimisation of evolution through genetic, pharmacological and technical human enhancement in the sense of transhumanism. Is transhumanism in view of this historical background with its different religious interpretations and narratives, as Francis Fukuyama found, "the World's Most Dangerous Idea" (10) or does it actually mark the end of a long journey?

It is difficult to answer this question because we cannot look into the future. But perhaps for the development of possible scenarios we can get support by the technology with its algorithms. They can open some doors into the future: They provide us with behavioural predictions, can trade for us on the stock exchange or make us look old on the display of our mobile phones. But it is only a matter of either creating technology and praising it, because it releases us from the burdens of nature – such as our greatest "inadequacy", mortality – or of fearing technology, because it can influence or even destroy nature – including our own?

One approach to solving these questions would be that technology is no longer seen as an opposite to nature, whereby this antithesis implies that machines have nothing to do with evolution and human nature. Rather, in the sense of Deleuze and Guattari, it would be conceivable to regard technology as a human production rooted in nature. Then social access to technology becomes a question of direct use and no longer the question of whether "it has always been like this". Such a task consists first of all in overriding the distinction between nature and culture by introducing concepts that are not provided for in this division. Thus, Deleuze and Guattari place corporeality in continuity with technology and thus embark on a search for the very place where bodily subjectivity is produced. For them, the unity of the body is conceived differently from the unity of the organism, namely as a unit of behavior and perception in which technical aids can be integrated (11).

While technology is understood as a product of humans, according to this view it can now be assumed that technology, as something already immanent to nature in general, must also be part of human nature. The use of technology is not something given by humans, but something that constitutes the *conditio humana*. Antonin Artaud already knew about immanence and pointed out that thinking is not innate but must be created in thinking (12). He knew that the problem is not to methodically direct or apply a preexistent thinking by nature and de jure, but to generate what does not exist. (13) But if we want to bear what does not exist, we cannot avoid the aspect of the performative. For it is only through the performative that the world is less repeated than created.

Gilles Deleuze and Felix Guattari also question Lacan's concept of the unconscious, which functions like a calculating machine, and replace it with their concept of the desire machine, which describes unconscious processes that cannot be modelled by any algorithm, however complex it will be. Performativity, coupled with an unconscious that, in contrast to psychoanalysis, is not linguistically structured, leads to something mechanical that is ultimately present in our body as well as in all areas of life: "It is at work everywhere, functioning smoothly at times, at other times in fits and starts. It breathes, it heats, it eats. It shits and fucks. What a mistake to have ever said the id." (14)

Associated with this abundance, immanence thus becomes the explication of being, even onthologie and finally the essence of 'expression' too, as Spinoza already used this term (15). If I do research for this book with a search engine and transfer the results into English via a translation program, it must also be clear to me as an author that in this process of reflection there was actually no really definable beginning and there will also be no end. The algorithms operating in the background, which support and relieve my thinking, also represent a certain determinism. Not for nothing means immanence, from an epistemological point of view such as that of Emanuel Kant, also staying within the limits of a possible experience (16).

Today, these limits are increasingly defined by machines with which we are closely connected and to which there are more and more points of reference. The bond becomes tighter and the leash shorter. Because also the journey of a thinking that is reproduced and published as a book, for example, also depends on search engines and may become nourishment for them later.

Insofar, our thinking about something is affected by exactly this "something". Technology is already immanent in the discourse about technology, its application and its possible consequences for our way of living as well as of thinking.

References:
1. cf. Ternes, Bernd (2016). Essay zur Technologie nach der Postmoderne mit besonderer Berücksichtigung des Satzes von Vilém Flusser: „Ich lebe so oft, wie ich durch Vernetzung an Verknotungen teilnehme". In: Kritiknetz - Zeitschrift für Kritische Theorie der Gesellschaft
2. cf. Shelley, Mary (2013). Frankenstein; or, The Modern Prometheus. Stuttgart, Reclam
3. cf. Canavero, Sergio (2017). Medicus magnus: Die Revolution der Medizin und wie wir sie für uns nützen. Wien, edition a
4. ibid
5. Descartes, René (2001). Bericht über die Methode. Ditzingen: Stuttgart, Reclam
6. cf. Hansemann, David (1899). Ueber das Gehirn von Hermann von Helmholtz. Leipzig, Zeitschrift für Psychologie und Physiologie der Sinnesorgane, Band 20, pp. 1 – 12
7. cf. Neumann, John (2014). Die Rechenmaschine und das Gehirn. München, Oldenbourg Wissensch. Vlg.
8. cf. Duschlbauer, Thomas (2019). Umdenken ist zu wenig. Graz, Wirtschaftsnachrichten Digitalreport, pp. 9 – 11
9. ibid, p. 11
10. Fukuyama, Francis (2004) Transhumanism: The World's Most Dangerous Idea. In: Foreign Policy 144, pp. 42 – 43
11. Deleuze, Gilles, Guattari Félix. (1974). Anti-Ödipus: Kapitalismus und Schizophrenie I. Frankfurt a.M, Suhrkamp, p. 7
12. Günzel, Stephan (1998): Immanenz. Zum Philosophiebegriff von Gilles Deleuze, Essen, p. 14
13. Deleuze, Gilles, Guattari Félix (1992). Tausend Plateaus. Kapitalismus und Schizophrenie II. Berlin, Merve Verlag, p 191 – 192
14. Deleuze, Gilles, Guattari Félix. (1974). Anti-Ödipus: Kapitalismus und Schizophrenie I. Frankfurt a.M., Suhrkamp, p. 1
15. cf. Deleuze, Gilles (1992). Expressionism in Philosophy: Spinoza. New York: Zone Books.
16. Kant, Immanuel (1998) Kritik der reinen Vernunft. Hamburg, Meiner Verlag, p. B 352 & 671

From dogma to style

In contrast to many other areas of business research, organisational research is characterised by a pronounced theoretical pluralism. On the one hand, this is due to the complexity of its object area. On the other hand, this is a typical feature of the social science style: There are fundamental differences in the approach to social science issues. Hardly any other social science research object has therefore produced such a broad diversity of theories as the organisation.

A critical analysis of the path from the "linguistic turn" to the "performative turn" requires, above all, an examination of postmodernist or post-structuralist theories around the organisation. They assume that organisations are above all defensive reactions to activities that threaten stability, which in view of a topic such as change management represents a paradox or means that change management takes on a system-stabilising function. However, this is no exception, since organisations in the sense of postmodernism generally represent indeterminacy and paradoxes (1).

Insisting on the fragility of the social corresponds with an interest in the mechanisms of stabilisation and the production of truth and meaning. For Michael Power (2), postmodernism is "an attack on unity," on the unity of the subject, the social, the text, and the organisation. He compares, for example, the "modernist" Habermas with the "postmodernist" Lyotard as typical representatives of the respective approaches. Habermas thus proceeds from the idea of the social consensus and attributes its emergence to individual action rationality (3). In this sense, an organisation is also an expression of such a consensus. Lyotard, on the other hand, believes in the indeterminacy of social structures that lack any rational basis. Consensus is regarded as an illusion, for there are no prerequisites for unity and understanding. Organisational research would therefore have to assume that there is no reliable description possibility as well as no generalizable model for organisations, because they lack any determinacy. Habermas' idea of consensus, quasi as a kind of artefact of communication, is for Lyotard an obsolete and suspect value. Consensus can be an intermediate step, but by no means a finality to be striven for.

Organisational theory in itself could be regarded as a language game in the sense of Lyotard. The empirical reality of organisational facts is shaped by the language habits and metaphors that have developed within the scientific communities. This language game has a tendency to become independent of empirical reality. The myth of the objectivity of scientific language conceals more unconscious than conscious metaphors that shape theory formation and analysis.

Sandelands and Drazin thus also criticise the tendency of many organisational researchers to leave the level of empirical reality in their choice of words. Instead, they would form their theories from abstract concepts such as "environment selection" or "strategic choice" in an almost mythologizing way, thus creating the illusion of representing processes that actually take place and can be traced through observation (4). This problem would be subject both to so-called endogenetic approaches, which explain structural changes through internal organisational decisions, and to exogenetic approaches, which see environmental factors as central causes for structural changes. The core of the problem is that the concepts of organisational theory describe a world that is beyond the direct experience of our senses. From their analysis, they derive the demand for a myth-free process theory (5) – and above all: They try to sensitise the organisation researchers regarding the use of language, particularly since knowledge in linguistic form is also the result of the research. Finally, somewhere else, namely in the current media discourse, it is emphasised in reference to Wittgenstein and Foucault that showing and speaking must be regarded as two separate symbolic orders and must therefore be clearly distinguished (6).

The interest in the significance of symbolic processes for the structure and dynamics of organisational action has thus led to the development of a special branch of research. Constructivism as a school based on Ludwig Wittgenstein, which places the linguistic constitution of reality in the foreground, forms a methodical background that is closely connected with the "linguistic turn", for example when it says: "The limits of my language mean the limits of my world."(7)

Since the Enlightenment, science has been exploring the world as an objective and quasi-human reality in order to gain knowledge. Everything that seemed subjective therefore had to be eliminated as far as possible in order to comply with this "purity law" in the cognitive process. In the 20th century, however, doubts about the unaffectedness of modern science arose from several sides. Physicists such as Einstein and Heisenberg recognised that observations have something relative about them and that observation also has an influence on what is observed (8), while there is the phenomenon of 2nd order observation, whereby "blind spots" become visible.

Ethnographers, too, recognised such interdependencies in their research, which was first expressed in structuralism and later in poststructuralism, which ultimately, with Foucault, questioned the causality of a knowledge that produced power. Rather, it is power that produces or permits a certain knowledge. At the same time, the focus is on forms of standardisation, discipline and the production of productive and 'instructive' subjects within organisations.

All these approaches to science that work with relations, blurriness, viewpoints, etc. have one thing in common: they take into account the aspect of a perspective taken by an observer. The world of radical constructivism in the sense of Heinz von Foerster, a nephew of Wittgenstein, is therefore always a world observed from a certain point of view, which is why we can conclude from the observations not only about the world, but also about the observer (9). It is this departure from objectivity and the backwardness of radical constructivism that opens up a wealth of possibilities for us in therapeutic and system-oriented work.

While realism assumed that the product of perception and observation should always be a representation or representation of things which, independently of the human subject, existed before this act as a knowledge to be discovered. Radical constructivism sees things as a construction of the observer in the act of knowledge and the environment as we perceive it as our invention (10).

Therefore, reality is nothing that already exists and is now waiting to be recognised and depicted by an individual. Unlike radical constructivism, which locates in the observer a machine-like cognitive apparatus that would act according to a calculable program, social constructivism now emphasises that the construction of reality is rather owed to a process of social interaction. One of human's peculiarities is his/her ability to communicate and, following the logic of constructivism, communication is not merely something that humans produce, but we ourselves are constituted by these acts as social beings (11).

Our reality is formed from our stories, especially since an individual is not related to him/herself but is integrated into social contexts. Postmodern theories also refer to this, beginning with Jean-François Lyotard, who defines narrative knowledge as a traditional knowledge in the form of stories and narratives. This knowledge does not require any deeper legitimation, which is why Lyotard, in the sense of postmodern pluralism, also emphasises the possibility of a juxtaposition of different perspectives, which can manifest themselves in language or – based on Ludwig Wittgenstein – in different language games (12). Such a constructivist theoretical approach, which consistently takes into account the existence of a multitude of observations, automatically results in a radically pluralistic position.

The view of organisation as an entity that is subject to internal laws independently of the individual actions of its members is transformed into a stronger emphasis on the role of the individual actor in the organisation. It is now seen less as a place of harmonious order than as arenas of conflicts of interest. The scepticism towards rules and laws, towards the "dogma", however, also helps an organisation to act more agilely in a rapidly changing environment with changing markets, new consumer needs, etc.

The approach to make use of chances and to permanently create new constellations of sense is mainly based on Wittgenstein's insights concerning language games, dogma and style as well as the phenomenon of fragmentation. It critically deals with all the dogmas in the area of creative or innovative processes from the point of view of knowledge management. Apart from this critique, Wittgenstein's ideas on style are also a reason why the activities concerning change employ aesthetic forms of articulation like e.g. hidden theatre and social sculptures to help us see the full range of actions that are available, to enhance and to optimally utilise them.

In this context it is important to emphasise that Wittgenstein is not teaching new concepts or making arguments in the first place, although much of what he writes certainly looks like those things; he is rather teaching us a skill, a method, a strategy. This method is precisely the method of destabilisation which rejects the idea of universal truths expressed by dogmata. Wittgenstein develops a radically devious style of writing in order to fracture the unities. By revealing all the contingency concealed by "normal" uses of words he tries to show how many different routes a discourse could possibly take. Usually normality bars our view of such routes. As a matter of fact, there is a profound interaction between normality – what Wittgenstein calls "ordinary language" – and philosophy (13).

In general, the current discourses on change within many organisations – even those which operate in an adhocratic way – are deeply dogmatic ones. The methods they employ are similar to those used by religion when it promises immediate salvation to those who assiduously participate in the transformative processes. In despite – or perhaps because – of the uncertainties of our time, change is not only an absolute term in the eyes of its managers but is also omnipresent and binding for all of us. Change represents what is good and/or necessary and has therefore become something that will always remain untainted. In the context of the dogma along with its KPIs, it is also something which we have to adapt to.

Complementary to this perspective, there is the sphere of style and the active creation or cocreation of new conditions. In our times it is no longer the size of an organisation that counts, but the process of reconfiguring its relationship with other organisations and the ability to build connections which radiate outwards. Beyond their functional and structural components organisations also have an aesthetic quality that is represented by the importance of myth and storytelling. By reconfiguring the interpretative context through which stakeholders perceive the organisation, it becomes possible to effect a change in the perceptions concerning the organisation with only minimal changes to the organisation itself.

For Roland Barthes, as well as for Ludwig Wittgenstein, style can be regarded as a permanent practice or the endless working on oneself. Style is the shaping of the picture of an individual in which this picture can be considered as an allegory. In contrast to a portrait – in which the spectrum of an interpretation is limited to the signified object and to at least one of its characteristics up to its complete identity with the model – the picture as an allegory can in every imaginable way be connected with what is derived from (14). This notion of style and picture is also expressed in one of Wittgenstein's reflections:

The effect of making men think in accordance with dogmas, perhaps in the form of certain graphic propositions, will be very particular: I am not thinking of these dogmas as determining men's opinions but rather as completely controlling the expression of all opinions. People will live under an absolute, palpable tyranny, thought without being able to say they are not free. I think the Catholic Church does something rather like this. For dogma is expressed in the form of an assertion, and it unshakeable, but at the same time any practical opinion can be made to harmonise with it; admittedly more easily in some cases than in others. It is not a wall setting limits to what can be believed, but more like a brake which, however, practically serves the same purpose; it's almost as though someone were to attach a weight to your foot to restrict your freedom of movement. This is how dogma becomes irrefutable and beyond reach of attack (15).

What Wittgenstein describes, certainly applies not only to religious organisations like the Catholic Church, but also to many other organisations. In this respect, the feeling expressed here is not surprising. Exciting, however, is the reference to the aspect of the imagery. The process of giving meaning to a dogma does not happen through its content but through its form or the pictoriality and vividness of a proposition. In contrast to its form, the content of a dogma does not constitute the individual attitude (16). With such radicalness, which is implied in this observation, we approach the heart of the discussion about rules in the Philosophical Investigations or respectively the paradox of the concept of rules:

201. This was our paradox: no course of action could be determined by a rule, because every course of action can be made out to accord with the rule. The answer was: if everything can be made out to accord with the rule, then it can also be made out to conflict with it. And so there would be neither accord nor conflict here. It can be seen that there is a misunderstanding here from the mere fact that in the course of our argument we give one interpretation after another; as if each one contented us at least for a moment, until we thought of yet another standing behind it. What this shews is that there is a way of grasping a rule which is not an interpretation, but which is exhibited in what we call "obeying the rule" and "going against it" in actual cases. Hence there is an inclination to say: every action according to the rule is an interpretation. But we ought to restrict the term "interpretation" to the substitution of one expression of the rule for another. (17)

Wittgenstein asks how it is possible that we are following rules if they do not "automatically" imply that they are obeyed in the sense of a causal determination or law of nature. If a rule exists to regulate something, then it simultaneously assumes the possibility of a contradictory behaviour. Therefore, the rule exists because of its contradiction, and exceptions to the rule are only the consequence of another interpretation. Later, Michel Foucault also remarks that a limit that could not be crossed would not exist; and that a crossing that would not cross a real border would only be an illusion (18). Without this interpretation we would not be able to understand the notion of regularity and within a system without different and also contradictory kinds of behaviour we do not have the occasion of reflecting the sense of a rule and consequently the rule itself.

This paradox is to be regarded as the result of the attempt to save the explanation as a useful methodological instrument and to bring the rule and its obedience into a certain relation through interpretation. But this implies that it becomes impossible to gain precisely the definite relation which was acknowledged in its existence before. Apparently, this special relation had to be denied as long as the presence of one interpretation refers to the absence of other interpretations (19).

In this context, Jacques Bouveresse presents a helpful distinction between a cause (as in the case of strict laws of nature) and motives (as in the nature of an interpretation). The motive is a kind of interpretation that we assign to our actions. This interpretation is surely not completely arbitrary, but it strongly depends on the – individual – way (of style) of "seeing". The motive makes our actions intelligible and endows them with meaning and the diversity of motives is in essence nothing else than the diversity of possible interpretations that come to our mind (also and especially through the presence of rules) when we attempt to understand our actions. Bouveresse concludes that "[...] in the language of Wittgenstein, the exploration of motives on the whole invokes the 'aesthetic' explanation in the larger sense than the causal explanation properly speaking." (20)

According to this notion, style cannot be derived from the knowledge of rules (Regelkenntnis) in a deductive way and therefore it cannot be imitated by simply obeying a particular set of rules. What is regulated by rules belongs to a universal sphere and style, which cannot be grasped by rules, belongs to the sphere of the individual. Insofar it is impossible to gain individuality out of the knowledge of rules, it is as such not universal and it is justified to argue that an individual style can be subsumed under the non-grammatical and paralinguistic means of expression (21).

A specific style produces artefacts that can be subjected to an aesthetic judgment. This judgment is based less on clearly comprehensible rules and laws but rather on certain principles which cannot be easily taught 1:1 and require additional explanation. We do not necessarily submit to those rules, we just apply these rules by using them. Specifically, artistic practice is based on a critical balance between conventional rule-following and exceptional rule-breaking (22).

Humankind mutates from a rational being to an imaginative being that is no longer in search of truth but style. The idea of style instead of truth sounds familiar when we think of Nietzsche who regarded absolute truth as something impossible and acknowledged the arts as its substitute too. For him, the only truth humankind is faced with is that it has to live without it (23).

Insofar, this approach makes the aesthetizising of truth possible – also in order to defend the plurality of different opinions and therein we maybe can see the formulation of Wittgenstein's basic idea: there are forms of representation which are independent of the content, as Wittgenstein says, and they determine the expression of opinions. These forms of representation are the pictorial propositions of a person. Due to this perspective, the identity of an individual is based on her/his style with this Wittgenstein implements a concept of style into anthropology which has originally been developed in the history of art (e.g. Wölfflin, Freyer): constraints of expression determine the human being or, in other words, style instead of truth becomes important for us as imaginative beings.

The search for truth or for an idea that is shared by all is proofed to be a hopeless attempt because norms and dogmas are automatically provoking deviation and heresy. Inquisition was an example for that: The clergy was able to discover a contradiction even in the affirmation of the dogma, because they knew it best and therefore gained access to the smallest scope for an interpretation that could be anticipated against the accused one. The interpretation of a dogma or a set of rules can be very individual and arbitrary. In the background are certain principles at work that emerge in the interpretation – possibly similar as in the case of an algorithm. Depending on how we interpret a rule we express a certain intention that objectively might not really match with the rule, but with our principles.

With rules we want to create liability, but on a meta-level and often in a very creative way our principles regulate how we ultimately interpret these rules. The rule is thus adapted to that certain sense which is sought by their compliance. As long as an individual principle prevails, the rule serves to reach a target through a structured and proven approach quickly and easily in practice. It is something like an accomplice helping us to shape the world according to our expectations. If rules are not pervaded by comprehensible principles and values, they are used in order to adapt us to their world. Then we lose control of the processes and become in the truest sense of the word "irresponsible", which usually results in the call for further and more stringent rules. The purpose of such rules often lies just in the aspect of compliance and not in the pursuit of an intention regarded as meaningful.

In this respect, style becomes a means to communicate the sense of the unintelligible because style is able to show meaning without postulating compulsory and universal rules for its understanding. This approach of an extreme aesthetic thinking would consequently lead to the abolition of the traditional limits between scientific discourse and artistic practice.

We need orientation and a certain degree of structure to follow an intention. Therefore, dogma and style do not exist as direct opposites, but style is merely a modification; it can be described as a renunciation of a universal intended image, which corresponds to the own personality. If style would be simply the opposite of dogma, it automatically would become dogmatic – and there are in fact examples where the violation of rules just ended in the creation of other rules.

One could be the "creative" practice of Design Thinking where in a lot of settings methods more and more became certain tools which supposedly need no further reflexion. At the beginning of Design Thinking, the focus was still on the cognitive processes that manifest themselves in different design activities. It had to be theoretically penetrated and explored. Meanwhile, Design Thinking has arrived in the corporate organisations, where it is not about gaining insight into creative processes, but rather about the problem-solving competence in virtually all areas of life. Insight thus becomes more and more a means to an end, whereas the creative breach of rules and the boundless release of human creativity ends in an activity within a tightly regulated structure with strict deadlines and a determined use of tools that could be compared with factory work at the beginning of the 20th century (24).

As style is located in the dimension of the process, we cannot predict its final destination that by all means could be a new dogma. In this respect, style is something "supplementary" in relation to the dogma in a Derridarian sense. It is complementary to something imperfect and acts at the same time as its replacement. Style is to some extend a dogma with a "human face".

In general, Wittgenstein describes not only human behaviour but also human thought as a phenomenon of style and his questioning of propositions becomes transformed into a question of form through his style-instead-of-truth thinking. One of the most evident examples for this shift can be found in his Tractatus. In its foreword we can read the following: "Its whole meaning could be summed up somewhat as follows: What can be said at all can be said clearly; and whereof one cannot speak thereof one must be silent." (25)

Obviously, the main problem Wittgenstein faced was the problem of drawing "a limit to thinking", a line between the meaningfully expressible and the inexpressible. The area of the expressible should be separated from the inexpressible. Therefore, it is necessary that both sides of the limit are accessible to thinking: "[...] for, in order to draw a limit to thinking we should have to be able to think both sides of the limit (we should therefore have to be able to think what cannot be thought)." (26)

Exactly this look on both sides were done by Gilles Deleuze and Félix Guattari in their last work "What is philosophy?" in a context that could be compared with our organisations. An organism represents, from their perspective, not the living, but rather embodies the restriction of the living. The organism as well as the organisation needs boundaries because according to Deleuze and Guattari what we fear the most is chaos or the abscond of thought. The desire for order and determination is the reason for the formation of an opinion with the help of marketing and its tools for communication like advertising and PR. Opinion is based on a simple reproducibility of perceptions and it insulates us from the chaos (27).

As an alternative to this shielding, Deleuze and Guattari prefer the open confrontation with the chaos because this process leads not only to the formation of an opinion but also of specific skills within an organisation. In their minds "thinking" means to compete with the chaos. This is also why the approach of performative change makes use of artistic stratagems. A work of art can be seen as a structure of sensations, affects and percepts which adds constancy to the becoming, makes invisible forces palpable and enables people to put something beyond their own existence. Mostly, it is not consent but excitement that leads us to new insights (28). Seen in this manner, it is not necessarily the organisation and socialisation of human beings that enables them to create artifacts, but rather the artifact may serve to bring people together and to enable them to acquire new competences.

Communication within organisations is still influenced by a means-purpose relationship or by the stimulus-response model of behaviourism. Communication has to be "useful", and in our eyes it is usually undertaken for a particular purpose. This is expressed, for example, in impact research, and the question how and to what extent communication changes our reality explores this relationship. According to his ideas on public relations, Jürgen Habermas has expressed this in the following manner: "Agreement" and "consensus" are the aims of communication, and therefore they must be subjected to certain comprehensible criteria, validity claims and rules of discourse. Among other critics, Michel Foucault does not solely locate discourse in linguistic practice and Jean-François Lyotard even went so far as to put the idea of the language game, conceived by Ludwig Wittgenstein, itself beyond consensus.

Wittgenstein uses this concept of a game as a means of comparison. Language games regulate our talking about the world through semantic and syntactic preconditions in their grammar. In this context, the idea of rules enables an authentic contemplation independently from causality and teleology. Moreover, it opens up a perspective beyond logic and explanation which is why we follow rules "blindly".

Therefore, Wittgenstein describes the language game as *das Hinzunehmende* which means that it is something that we have to accept or to take for granted (29) and he regards language "as a practice involving various skills and forms of knowledge rather than language as a deep structure of rules which could be reduced to theoretical knowledge (episteme)" (30). Language seems to have lost its two main functions, namely representation and legitimation, respectively both have collapsed into each other. We can now choose between the following "alternatives": either we keep the everyday contradictions and inconsistencies like a 'confveve' tweet by Donald Trump, or we make it comfortable in the petting zoo of simple tautologies and become so receptive to manipulation: "When you talk about George Bush – I mean, say what you want, the World Trade Center came down during his time," said Donald Trump in a simple but towards his followers quite convincing way, in order to kick out his former opponent Jeb Bush in the running for the presidential election by discrediting him as a member of the Bush family (31).

Central for this concept is also Wittgenstein's fragmentary style of writing because it corresponds with many aspects of his philosophy (e.g. questions of plurality, his aesthetic judgements etc.) Style functions as a connection between the sayable and the unsayable, and the fragmentary style – as Wittgenstein makes use of it – can be regarded as something which ironically tries to represent the unrepresentable.

In this respect, Wittgenstein shares a long tradition: According to Manfred Frank, Wittgenstein's texts are fragments failing to belong to a wholeness which actually cannot presented in the field of logical and calculated propositions because of the grammar of its language games. Therefore, these fragments are related – presumably unwillingly – to the tradition of early Romantic philosophy (32). For example, for Schlegel it was the most important task for philosophy to express the infinite although he is aware that it is only possible to say something limited. If one simultaneously has to respect the limits of the sayable but nevertheless wants to transgress them, one has to make perceptible what is said as something which was not actually meant. This is the case in irony which is no pragmatic-syntactic means but a stylistic one. One says something special but in such a way that it suggests one could mean something different. One has to sacrifice the appearance of the ultimate in order to say something infinite (33).

In the context of an organisation that also defines itself through the recognition of formal rules of its members, irony may fulfil a function that goes beyond these formal expectations, but it may even stabilise them by enabling communication in certain situations in the first place. Networked and automated systems for decision making, be they digitally supported or engineered, complicate or even make this man-made solution in dealing with contradictory purposes impossible.

In general, irony is the difference between saying and meaning, and philosophy becomes ironic insofar as on the one hand it is fixed to certain ideals and on the other hand it is in doubt of their existence and content but unable to replace the old ideals by new ones. We can find such irony, for example, in the Tractatus when Wittgenstein at first claims that he has solved the essential problems of philosophy and the calls philosophy as such in question and tells us that none of our problems is solved (34). The ironic strategy consists in pre-programming a misunderstanding, which is exactly the reason why we have become aware of the real problems; why we begin to ask different questions.

Concerning the paradox of rules the great potential for organisations can be seen in giving up the idea of a fixed identity and a certain internal logic in favour of a vision of an organisation that is constantly redefining itself in order to be able to shape their own future. For this kind of rule breaking on a strategic level we can say that every interpretation of a rule – also following its obvious intention – has an inherent potential for change. Therefore, sub-version can also take place exactly where a rule is followed in the most accurate way. Meticulous compliance or the over-acceptance of a senseless rule can be regarded as a guerilla stratagem and may lead to the same chaotic conditions as the breach of a practical rule.

Obviously, there are parallels between the romantic irony and Wittgenstein's notion of style. In general, irony is also one of the most effective weapons, because it leads often to nothing than the effect of "disarming" an opponent. This is true for the rhetorical irony, whereas the romantic irony is capable of much more, because as an aesthetic theory it is not only dedicated to the work itself, but also to the conditions under which it is created. Not the "new" as a product – or in the case of the arts as creation – is in the foreground, but also the process of coming into being, and generally the conditions of production are discussed. They become part of the result and they are telling a story.

In its own inexplicit and ironic way, the fragmented character of Wittgenstein's texts also refers to a political and historical dimension. For Wittgenstein, fragmentation is not only connected with the object of his thinking, it also reveals an intuitive understanding of the time when he made use of his style (35). Ironically, the potential of such a fragment lies in the fact that its potential cannot completely exploited and therefore there are different links for connections. Fragments are open in its vagueness and therefore they are the scopes for different interpretations.

Digital processes generate digital data, which is attributed the potential to be powerful innovation drivers and problem solvers. Thus, they create their own reality by suggesting a coherent whole (36). This ordered, coherent whole appears to be the ideal basis for rational decision-making: the answer lies, so to speak, in the data. This gives the impression that actual decision making becomes almost obsolete. Because if you know everything and have an overview of everything, you can simply calculate the best solution. The rhetorical figure that "the data speaks for itself" will continue to gain importance in organisations. Who wants to oppose smart recommendations? Who takes the risk of deciding against "better" knowledge? Who wants to open the barrel in the meeting and question this so beautifully ordered, so clearly and helpfully pre-structured decision situation (37)?

At the same time, an opposite trend is emerging: there is a rumbling in the organisation's machinery, because digitalisation produces new coordination requirements. Anyone who takes a close look at setting up a highly automated production process will notice that many automation processes only work because employees spend a lot of creativity every day to deal with the pitfalls of automation (38).

No matter how large the amount of data may be, a fundamental law of organizing cannot be shaken: decisions must be made – still under the conditions of limited rationality (39). They can be automated, but this does not make organisations more rational because they buy new blind spots. These "pre-programmed" frictional losses are often ignored by the proponents of smart tools, according to the motto: Who needs superiors if the solution is served on a silver platter by digitisation and why hierarchies if the project seems to be the new form of organisation par excellence? Agile projects want to throw off the shackles of hierarchy, decision-making responsibility should fluctuate freely between colleagues. The better idea wins. An enchanting performance. And not an unknown one: The idea that less formal structure is synonymous with gaining freedom is as old as false. Just because something is not formally regulated, we are not dealing with an empty page, a tabula rasa or free space. Informal expectations are formed, which regulate what is decided by whom and how: Whose admonition is to be listened to, and who is only over-cautious? Who is simply ambitious, and who is overshooting the mark with their idea? The agile machine purrs as long as it runs informal, i.e. as long as goals are achieved, conflicts are capped or resolved informally, and as long as everyone feels they are equally committed (40).

Apart from Wittgenstein, there are some similar attempts to propagate and use fragmentation as a means for critique against the myth of the universal. In this respect one can think of Adorno who follows the Kantian tradition by claiming that: "Only a philosophy in fragment form would give their proper place to the monads, those illusory idealistic drafts. They would be conceptions, in the particular, of the totality that is inconceivable as such." (41)

Here another component of irony is revealed, which serves as a means to have an assumption of entireness and therefore can be interpreted as an expression of our necessarily limited being in a virtual infinite fullness of life. Irony is therefore also something of a processing strategy towards the countless options which we are faced with in life today and which permanently compel us to make decisions, or even worse, leave us clueless without being able to make a decision. For whatever we decide, there is always a bitter aftertaste because at the same time we also decided against many other options – maybe the better ones. However, this wealth of possibilities offered in our era of globalisation is, of course, also a key to change and innovation by intelligently linking things or transferring them to a different context.

However, in times of digitalisation irony has a hard destiny. After all, to achieve quotas has long been an integral part of any statement: Many can't resist the fact that their internal algorithm, which always strives for confirmation, synchronises itself with the algorithms that want to generate high interaction rates via likes and dislikes. Accordingly, we tend to make statements with the lowest ambiguity because they have been proven to have the highest probability of success. And if irony lives from something, then from ambiguity. Especially winkersmileys and other labels for 'irony off' are a good sign that we take the risk less and less and slowly but surely forget the irony.

But there are also situations where we become not aware of different possibilities and options although they are still existent. In his essay on "différance" Jacques Derrida calls this phenomenon "silent irony". It happens when – due to a violation of an orthographic rule – we are not able to hear the transgression. Derrida describes "différance" as strategic and bold. It is strategic because no transcentental and outside the field of writing located truth is able to dominate the totality of the field in a theological way. And it is bold because this strategy is not a simple strategy in a sense that we are saying that strategy is driving tactics according to an ultimate purpose, a telos or a motif of dominance and the final reoccupancy of the movement and the field. It is a strategy without an aim, a blind tactic or an empiric errantry. This errantry at the sign of "différance" does not follow either a philosophical-logical discourse nor its opposite, an empiric-logical discourse. That's why Derrida introduces the term "play" and refers to Ferdinand de Saussure, who made the arbitrariness of the sign and its differential character to a principle of general semiology and especially of linguistics (42).

In this context, it may be helpful to think of Derrida as one who is setting forth a language game in the way it is manifested in Wittgenstein's Philosophical Investigations. From this perspective, Derrida is laying out a sense of his basic agenda through the cultivation of an ensemble of motifs, metaphors and tactical analyses in order to illuminate a thought which he wishes to convey to the reader. Simultaneously, with the subversion of the authorial presence that is undertaken in his text on "différance", the very attempt to communicate to the reader will necessarily be subverted also, and Derrida intimates this possibility when he intimates that the motif of "différance" itself will have to be deleted (43).

In the deconstructive proof of what is "suppressed" or imperceptible in the discourse, the unity of the organisation in its severity, purity and closure is undermined. The proof of this logic of opposition is followed by the revaluation of the suppressed concepts, etc., which, with the dominant assertions or assumptions of the considered discourse, enter into a new and continued game of differences (44). For organisational research following Derrida, the specific configurations of the simultaneity of closure and opening of structures, of the fixation and destabilisation of meaning must then be examined and subjected to a deconstructive consideration. Derrida's critical commitment to organisational research is thus also to lend a voice and legitimacy to the forms of knowledge that are not articulated in discourse, but nevertheless substantiate them (45).

Derrida suggests that meaning resides in the interrelation of the signs which are operative within the general economy of the text, of the place of polysemy beyond the restricted economy of a privileged language game that is dominating as the proper meaning. This playfulness, which is meant to be disruptive and subversive, can be regarded as a motif which intimates a play that, as Derrida claims, is prior to being, and the ontological difference between beings and being (46). It may also be applied to what is regarded as "guerilla", not in its original meaning as a kind of warfare but as a practice based on artistic style.

Originally, the term was established at the beginning of the 19th century, during the War of Independence between Spain and Portugal on the one side and Napoleon on the other. Small groups of irregulars thereby inflicted heavy losses on the French troops.

Guerilla employs small and manageable amounts of resources, divides the war into a series of smaller skirmishes and utilises pinprick tactics to determine when and where these conflicts will occur. This is necessary, as the success or failure of these battles largely determines which further steps will be taken. After each step, an analysis of the situation is carried out. The lessons thereby learned influence the course of future activities.

Although this kind of guerilla seems to be inherently socially romantic, especially since it involves the elimination of despotic regimes, we must not forget that it is still a kind of warfare. In war, the dignity and the life of a person have no importance.

Therefore, it is quite a serious matter when various stratagems of warfare are trained at management and leadership seminars without any reflection as to their totalitarian background. It is debatable whether doing so is a good idea (47).

On the other hand, there is another approach to this phenomenon which does not focus on resistance but rather on contradiction. It is not primarily based on dogmas but to a much greater extent on artistic styles, even though both approaches originate from similar conditions and make use of comparable stratagems. In his artistic intervention "Please love Austria" ("Bitte liebt Österreich") which took place in front of the Vienna State Opera, Christoph Schlingensief emphasised that the time of simple resistance is over and that contradiction now is necessary. Art cannot contribute to improving politics. The artist can merely create an image that has to be accepted as it is (48).

This example of artistic intervention in a public space made it clear that resistance, as such, cannot work; in our complex world it is often not even clear who the opponents are. Resistance movements would quickly break up into factions. Only by creating a contradictory situation does the whole range of diverging interests, points of view, meanings and attitudes become obvious, because this kind of guerilla does not simply differentiate between friend and foe. The presented fragments of society should not be considered in isolation from each other but rather interconnected in a number of different manners. That automatically increases the degree of complexity and contradiction. We have to be able to bear this level of tension, or to reduce the tension by precisely analysing differences and negotiating between them (49).

By abandoning the notion that art is resistance, Schlingensief moreover indicates that the production of works of art cannot be positioned outside of society. Aesthetics does not follow the stereotype of the de-ranged (verrückt) artist. It also does not create misunderstood martyrs. On the contrary, the aesthetic experience has to be regarded as a form of mediation, which can no longer be experienced within the framework of conventional means of communication. The reason why this form of art is seen as subversive and threatening is not because it takes place in "catacombs", outside of society, but precisely because it suddenly emerges in the centre of events and thus radically disrupts the continuity of our experiences. It does not focus on altering our convictions but on creating affects; it creates a rough draft of what is possible.

Pure invention in the field of performative change can be compared to Utopia in the sphere of art. Invention also defies reasoning initially and should not be mixed up with "fake news" or the creation of the so-called "alternative facts". Jean-François Lyotard cites a prominent example from science. In his "Beyond the Pleasure Principle", Sigmund Freud proposed that death instincts have permeated life instincts. He could not logically convince anybody – not even himself – of the truth of this idea. To justify this theory, Freud developed a coherent approach, thereby making use of a set of quite uncommon sources: philosophers, poets and biologists. In his paper he frankly admitted that his theory could be compared to a dilapidated building. In fact, it was a kind of theory fiction, in which the power of invention was allowed free rein. Lyotard maintains that it arises from a passionate apathy. Out of scientific curiosity the "new" became an object of desire, and that made Freud a monster in the sense of de Sade. Freud did not follow the pathos of theory but rather the pathos of the incommunicable singularity. In a cool manner he pursued the course of his idea and succeeded in confirming his personal inclinations. He candidly admits to having done so. He refused to be confined by Wittgenstein's dictate "Whereof one cannot speak, thereof one must be silent." Nevertheless, Freud was not opposed to theory, and did not attempt to flee from it. He merely tried to thwart it in a playful manner and to parody it (50).

Our manner of thinking can be regarded as a journey and there are many who ask us to stop and terminate this nomadism. Many people say that we should only talk about things we understand, and that we should not say anything about, and not even think about, things that we don't understand. But who defines what we understand, and do we really want to exclusively devote our lives to "understanding", to this most convenient form of deadlock? Real change is usually beyond the ordinary, beyond what is generally understood. The more we learn about something, the more we want to know about it and become aware of the boundary between the things that can be spoken about and the unspeakable. This is an important landmark but not a fixed constant. Instead, it is something that can be expanded and pushed forward in front of us. We gain experience and expand the horizon of the experiences that lie before us – that is what also performative change within organisation may be all about (51).

This concept of application can itself be understood as a deconstructive intervention that undermines the dualistic opposition of 'basic research' and 'applied research' - and thus also the 'problem-solving orientation' attributed to the so-called 'applied' disciplines. There are neither secured foundations from which knowledge is derived 'from above' or 'from below', nor are there 'neighbouring disciplines' from which 'secured knowledge' could be imported in order to cement an existing foundation.

There is only knowledge, protected from reflection, that allows to build the – perhaps necessary – fictions that enable existence and action. What we consider knowledge is based on this "harmony of deceptions" (52). It describes precisely what is conceivable and what is unthinkable.

It is also quite conceivable that Ludwig Wittgenstein, one of the protagonists of the 'lingustic turn', also anticipated a concept of application or even the 'performative turn' in his work. In the very first sentences of his first publication, the Tractatus logico-philosophicus, when he postulates "The world is all that is the case" and immediately continues: "The world is the totality of facts, not of things". For the early Wittgenstein the world thus "disintegrates" into facts and "What is the case – a fact – is the existence of states of affairs." So things are inherent in facts and they can occure in states of affaires, which is why there must be the possibility that the facts are already prejudiced in the things and why the objects contain the possibility of all facts (53). Starting from what is conceivable, the application of things would ultimately also reveal their possibilities or the 'behavior' of the things in the facts.

An explicit term "performative" in connection with the classification of sentences does not appear until Austin, but already Wittgenstein, after his departure from logical empiricism, paid attention in his philosophical investigations to an aspect of the performative speech act in the context of his determination of language games (54). Thus, Ludwig Wittgenstein's late philosophy anchors individual mental states in a collective practice of common behavior in a movement comparable to pragmatism. Therefore, meaning or even individual intentions are culturally and practically established (55). In spite of all the strength to transcend the given, according to this view also the human mind remains "constitutive", as it is often said in a very abbreviated manner, bound to this reality.

Wittgenstein imagines a primitive language in the philosophical studies in which two people operate in a hierarchical relationship with each other, so that the assistant B brings the desired article to the builder A upon his exclamation "slab!" (56) After he has dealt with the various functions of words, the process of learning a language and the concept of the "language game", Wittgenstein returns to the example again in § 19 and pursues the question of whether "slab!" is a shortening of "Bring me a slab!" (57) According to Wittgenstein, it is difficult to determine what this difference is between the statement "five slabs" and the command "five slabs!" Thus, the difference could lie in the pronunciation, the tone, on the other hand there are many different possibilities of the pronunciation, whereby the difference could be limited purely to the use (58). The same statement can be used thus once statically, once performatively; the differentiation seems difficult

The relationship between name and nominee can, among many other possibilities, also consist in the fact that hearing the name calls the image of the nominee to our souls (59). Judith Butler will, in the broadest sense, include this approach in her concept of invocation, even if she expands it, so that not only the image of the nominee is called to the soul, but the nominee itself will constitute through the invocation. Jens Kertschner has also pointed out that Wittgenstein, in his Philosophical Investigations, moves language into the vicinity of a theatrical concept of performativity in the sense of performance as staging (60).

Wittgenstein's sentences for instruction, however, in contrast to the later approaches to performativity, fall under the concept of performance, since they presuppose an acting subject. Since this subject belongs to a certain form of life, language is also dependent on it. It is thus also determined by a familiarisation with a society. In addition, there is the aspect of corporeality, since the body language that accompanies verbal articulation or even sends signals without its influence can never be completely guided by the speaker (61).

Focusing on digitisation within organisations, however, we must not forget that Wittgenstein did not only have an affinity for technology merely from his educational background, but that his Philosophical Investigations – especially his concept of language games – also deal with the use of language as a kind of tool. Coeckelbergh and Funk address these parallels between language and technology in the context of performance: "Another way of making this point and apply Wittgenstein's remarks on language and tool use to thinking about technology in general is to use the concept of 'performance'." For them, Wittgenstein's understanding of language as well as his very methodology in the Investigations and other writings can be interpreted as centring on performance, understood as meaningful and successful practice – whether linguistic or technological (62).

In view of this, Wittgenstein, whose work is considered to have a high degree of timelessness, can be seen not only as a forerunner of the performative, but also as a forerunner of technical change. Even the processes of standardisation and unification were not hidden from Wittgenstein. In the foreword to his "Philosophical Investigations", for example, he distinguishes between two different existential attitudes, technology and contemplation, which for him face each other. Our techno-civilisation thus represents a Zeitgeist that is confronted with a spirit of contradiction (63).

In "Culture and Value" (Vermischte Bemerkungen) it also becomes clear that Wittgenstein was critical of the cultural changes and a way of thinking that was shaped by the belief in the progress of technical-scientific civilisation and brought with it a loss of artistic taste. Although this style of thinking was certainly repulsive to him, he never condemned it as immoral, because he believed that the disappearance of a culture was not synonymous with the disappearance of human values (64).

Apart from this distinction between the terms "culture" and "value", which is important when considering an organisation, the question also arises as to how much the language games of the members of an organisation are affected or even switched off in some places as a result of technological change. Wittgenstein, for example, with his "family resemblance", also introduced a perspective that shows that concepts can be blurred and are based on paradigmatic use cases. An analysis is not necessary to be able to master or explain them (65). On the other hand, however, in companies, digital technologies are used to try to eliminate all vagueness and ambiguity, and digital communication also reduces the opportunities for informal exchange of knowledge. Management consultants, too, see themselves more obliged to act like engineers and to eradicate different interpretations with the help of technical devices than to deal with the conceptual and symbolic peculiarities of language within a company. Additionally, the frequently drawn distinction between technical and social innovation misses the point that technical innovation always changes social practices and, conversely, new social practices also lead to the emergence of new technologies. If, for example, people had not become increasingly mobile in their everyday work and leisure time in the past century through cars and airplanes etc., the particularly urgent need to invent a mobile phone would probably not have arisen either.

References:
1. cf. Power, Michael (1990). Modernism, postmodernism management and organization. In: J. Hassard & D. Pym (Hrsg.), The theory and philosophy of organizations. Critical issues and new perspectives (Social analysis). London: Routledge, pp. 109 – 124
2. ibid, p. 110
3. cf. Habermas, Jürgen (1981). Theorie des kommunikativen Handelns. (Bd. 1: Handlungsrationalität und gesellschaftliche Rationalisierung, Bd. 2: Zur Kritik der funktionalistischen Vernunft), Frankfurt a.M., Suhrkamp
4. cf. Sandelands, Lloyd & Drazin, Robert (1989). On the Language of Organization Theory. Organization Studies, Vol. 10, pp. 457 – 477
5. ibid, p. 472

6. Mersch, Dietmar (2002). Was sich zeigt. Materialität, Präsenz, Ereignis. München, Wilhelm Fink Verlag, p. 136 & p. 239

7. Wittgenstein, Ludwig (1963). Tractatus logico-philosophicus. Frankfurt a. M., Suhrkamp, p. 89

8. Watzlawick, Paul. (2002). Einleitung. In: Krieg, Peter & Watzlawick Paul (Hrsg.). Das Auge des Betrachters. Beiträge zum Konstruktivismus. Heidelberg, Carl-Auer-Systeme Verlag, p. 8

9. ibid, p. 9

10. Glasersfeld, Ernst von (2002). Abschied von der Objektivität. In: Krieg, Peter & Watzlawick Paul (Hrsg.). Das Auge des Betrachters. Beiträge zum Konstruktivismus. Heidelberg, Carl-Auer-Systeme Verlag, p. 18

11. Schlippe, Arist von & Schweitzer, J. (2016). Lehrbuch der systemischen Therapie und Beratung I und II. Göttingen, Vandenhoeck & Ruprecht, p. 122

12. Lyotard, Jean-François (1984). The Postmodern Condition: A Report on Knowledge. Minneapolis, University of Minnesota Press, pp. 41 – 43

13. Staten, Henry (1985). Wittgenstein and Derrida. Oxford, Basil Blackwell, pp. 66 – 75

14. Barthes, Roland (1977). Writing Degree Zero. Selected and trans. Annette Leavers & Colin Smith, New York, Hill and Wang, p. 11

15. Wittgenstein, Ludwig (1994). Vermischte Bemerkungen. Frankfurt a. M., Suhrkamp, Ms 118 86v, p. 64

16. Wiesing, Lambert (1992). Pluralität durch ästhetisches Denken. In: Postmoderne oder das Ende des Suchens. Eggingen, Edition Isele, p. 120

17. Wittgenstein, Ludwig (1953). Philosophical Investigations. Trans. G.E.M. Anscomb, Oxford, Basil Blackwell, § 201

18. Foucault, Michel (1974). Vorrede zur Überschreitung. In: Von der Subversion des Wissens. Hg. u. übers. v. Walter Seitter. München, Hanser, p. 37

19. Ohler, Matthias (1990). Sprachphilosophie oder Sprachwissenschaft? In: Fritz Wallner & Arne Haselbach (Ed.). Wittgensteins Einfluß auf die Kultur der Gegenwart. Philosophica 9, Wien, Wilhelm Braumüller, p. 30

20. Bouveresse, Jacques (1995). Wittgenstein reads Freud, The myth of the unconscious. Princeton, Princeton University Press, pp. 78 – 81

21. Frank, Manfred (1989). Einführung in die frühromantische Ästhetik, lectures. Frankfurt a. M., Suhrkamp, p. 30

22. Bauer, Robert (2007). Organizations as Orientation Systems – Some Remarks on the Aesthetic Dimension of Organizational Design. Michael Shamiyeh, (Ed.). In Organizing for Change. Integrating architectural thinking into other fields. Basel, Birkhäuser, pp. 34 – 46

23. Heller, Erich (1988). The importance of Nietzsche: ten essays. Chicago/London, University of Chicago Press, p 153

24. Seitz, Tim (2017). Design Thinking und der neue Geist des Kapitalismus. Bielefeld, transcript, p 113 – 125

25. Wittgenstein, Ludwig (1963). Tractatus logico-philosophicus, Frankfurt a. M., Suhrkamp, p. 7

26. ibid, p. 27

27. Deleuze, Gille & Guatarri Felix (1991). Was ist Philosophie? Frankfurt a. M., Suhrkamp, pp. 220 – 229

28. ibid, pp. 220 – 229
29. Wittgenstein, Ludwig (1953). Philosophical Investigations. Trans. G.E.M. Anscomb, Oxford, Basil Blackwell, §§ 217-219
30. Steuerman, Emilia (1992). Habermas vs. Lyotard: Modernity vs. Postmodernity. In: Judging Lyotard, Benjamin, A. (Ed.), London/New York, Routledge, p. 114
31. Francis, Davies (2015). Trump on President Bush and 9/11: 'The World Trade Center Came Down During His Reign'. link (07.20.2020): https://foreignpolicy.com/2015/10/16/trump-on-president-bush-and-911-the-world-trade-center-came-down-during-his-reign/
32. Frank, Manfred (1989a). Wittgensteins Gang in die Dichtung. In: Manfred Frank & Gianfranco Soldati, (Ed.), Wittgenstein. Literat und Philosoph. Pfullingen, Neske, pp. 31 – 32
33. ibid, p. 3
34. Stern, Josef P. (1990). Literarische Aspekte der Schriften Ludwig Wittgensteins. In: Wittgenstein und. Wendelin Schmidt-Dengler, Martin Huber & Michael Hutter (Ed.), Wien, Edition S., p. 28
35. Schulz, Walter (1979). Wittgenstein: Die Negation der Philosophie. Neske, Pfullingen, p. 11
36. cf. Heintz, Bettina (2016). Welterzeugung durch Zahlen. Modelle politischer Differenzierung in internationalen Statistiken. 1948 – 2010. Soziale Systeme, 18 (1 – 2), pp. 7 – 39
37. Büchner, Stefanie; Kühl, Stefan & Muster Judith (2017). Ironie der Digitalisierung. Weswegen Steuerungsphantasien zu kurz greifen. Working Paper 13/2017, Universität Bielefeld, p. 1
38. ibid, p. 2
39. cf. Simon, Herbert A. (1959). Theories of decision making in economics and behavioural science. In: American Economic Review, Vol. 49, Nr. 3, pp. 253 – 283
40. Büchner, Stefanie; Kühl, Stefan & Muster Judith (2017). Ironie der Digitalisierung. Weswegen Steuerungsphantasien zu kurz greifen. Working Paper 13/2017 Universität Bielefeld, pp. 2 – 3
41. Adorno, Theodor W. (1973). Negative Dialectics. Trans. E.B. Ashton, London, Routledge & Kegan, p. 36
42. Derrida, Jacques (1993). Die Différance. In: Postmoderne und Dekonstruktion. Stuttgart, Reclam, pp 76 – 81
43. Luchte, James (2016). Mortal Thought. London, Bloomsbury, pp. 164 – 167
44. cf. Linstead, Stephen (2004). Organisation Theory and Postmodern Thought. New York, Sage
45. Chia, Robert (2003). Organization Theory as a Postmodern Science. Oxford, The Oxford Handbook of Organization Theory, p. 127
46. Luchte, James (2016). Mortal Thought. London, Bloomsbury, pp. 164 – 167
47. Duschlbauer, Thomas, Lanz, Walter & Hattmannsdorfer, Armin. (2013). Innovationsguerilla. St. Gallen/Zürich, MidasManagement, p. 59 – 64
48. Schlingensief, Christoph (2006). Ausländer Raus! DVD documentation, producer Paul Poet, Wien, Hoanzl
49. Duschlbauer, Thomas, Lanz, Walter & Hattmannsdorfer, Armin. (2013). Innovationsguerilla. St. Gallen/Zürich, MidasManagement, p. 72

50. Lyotard, Jean-François (1979). Apathie der Theorie. Berlin, Merve, p. 43
51. Duschlbauer, Thomas, Lanz, Walter & Hattmannsdorfer, Armin. (2013). Innovationsguerilla. St. Gallen/Zürich, MidasManagement, pp. 70 – 72
52. Fleck, Ludwik (1980). Entstehung und Entwicklung einer wissenschaftlichen Tatsache: Eine Einführung in die Lehre vom Denkstil und Denkkollektiv. Frankfurt a.M., Suhrkamp, p 41
53. Wittgenstein, Ludwig (1963). Tractatus logico-philosophicus. Frankfurt a. M., Suhrkamp, p. 11
54. cf. Wittgenstein, Ludwig (1953). Philosophical Investigations. Trans. G.E.M. Anscomb, Oxford, Basil Blackwell, § 23
55. cf. Volbers, Jörg (2017). Die offene Praxis der Sprache. Wittgensteins und Austins pragmatische Wende der Sprachphilosophie. In: Bedorf/Gerlek (Eds.): Philosophien der Praxis, pp. 141 – 179
56. cf. Wittgenstein, Ludwig (1953). Philosophical Investigations. Trans. G.E.M. Anscomb, Oxford, Basil Blackwell, § 2
57. cf., § 19
58. cf., § 21
59. cf., § 37
60. Kertschner, Jens (2003). Wittgenstein- Austin- Derrida. „Performativität" in der sprachphilosophischen Diskussion. In: Jens Kertscher & Dieter Mersch (Hg.): Performativität und Praxis. München, Wilhelm Fink Vlg., p. 40
61. ibid, p. 41
62. Austin, John L. (1972). Zur Theorie der Sprechakte. Stuttgart, Reclam, p. 35
63. Wittgenstein, Ludwig (1964). Philosophische Bermerkungen. Frankfurt a.M., Suhrkamp, p. 4
64. Schulte, Joachim (1990). Chor und Gesetz: Wittgenstein im Kontext. Frankfurt a.M., Suhrkamp, p. 60
65. Buchholz, Kai (2000). Sémantique formelle et ressemblances de famille. In: Logique et Analyse. 4, pp 345 – 356

From the ready-made opinion to the scope of action

If an understanding of the concept of organisation – as already explained – depends on organising the understanding, then according to a systemic view one cannot organise the understanding at all in too many different ways (1). This also means that, based on the already described phenomenon of immanence, we do not necessarily have to generate new data for an analysis of topics such as representation and legitmation within an organisation, but can make already existing sources effective in a new sense. While digital technologies such as big data are more or less contributing to the oblivion of history, we are allowed to sit back on the cushion of traditional knowledge and look for new contexts and insights that will help us understand change within an organisation better. After all, change or something new directly raises two essential questions that are closely related to the main two functions of language – representation and legitimation: What is that? And what is it for? In order to do justice to such questions concerning change, we must also deal with the truth and truthfulness of the answers demanded.

A frequently used term that is introduced into the discourse about representation and legitimation is "authenticity". For example, managers should act in an authentic way and internal communication must be authentic too. Authenticity represents, as we shall see later, a truth. But truthfulness goes on. Truthfulness also means saying things we think our counterparts won't like so much. Truthfulness is something deeply individual because it means staying true to oneself instead of always fulfilling the expectations of others – and: truthfulness is closely linked to the concept of immanence.

With regard to this concept, Gilles Deleuze and Felix Guatarri are of the opinion that Spinoza was the "prince of philosophy" because he was the first to succeed in thinking substance entirely from the idea of immanence (2): *"Spinoza was the philosopher who knew full well that immanence was only immanent to itself and therefore that it was a plane traversed by movements of the infinite, filled with intensive ordinates. He is therefore the prince of philosophers. Perhaps he is the only philosopher never to have compromised with transcendence and to have hunted it down everywhere."* (3)

However, the idea of immanence – leading to a certain concept of style – had already found enthusiastic supporters much earlier. Among them was

Johann Wolfgang von Goethe, who not only admired Spinoza's ideas, but also incorporated them into his work, thus obviously influencing Ludwig Wittgenstein later. If we apply the concept of immanence – in the sense of Deleuze – to an analysis of technology and regard technology as immanent in nature, then it is not unimportant that it is also reflections on nature that Goethe made in relation to this concept, as we will see in this chapter.

In 1812, Goethe wrote this verse in "Prooemion" in the spirit of Spinoza, whereby this poem is to be seen as one of the clearest allusions to immanence:

> Was wär ein Gott, der nur von außen stieße,
> Im Kreis das All am Finger laufen ließe!
> Ihm ziemt's, die Welt im Innern zu bewegen,
> Natur in Sich, Sich in Natur zu hegen,
> So dass, was in Ihm lebt und webt und ist,
> Nie Seine Kraft, nie Seinen Geist vermisst.
> What God would outwardly alone control,
> And on His finger whirl the mighty Whole?
> He loves the inner world to move, to view
> Nature in Him, Himself in Nature too,
> So that what in Him works, and is, and lives,
> The measure of His strength, His spirit gives. (4)

Later, in the year 1829, his poem "Vermächtniß" (Testament) appeared, in which Goethe also creates a reference through a metaphor of nature, which – starting from Spinoza's concept of immanence – creates a bridge to performativity. Goethe himself took a stand on this work insofar as he placed it in the historical context of the Napoleonic Wars and thus alluded to the weakening of the Germans as a nation. For him, following the example of the English, the Germans would have been helped if they had been taught less philosophy and more energy, less theory and more practice. (5)

The following verse from this poem is devoted to our trust in our senses as well as in the question of truth, which Goethe answers for himself insofar as fruitfulness alone is true.

Und war es endlich dir gelungen,
Und bist du vom Gefühl durchdrungen:
Was fruchtbar ist allein ist wahr;
Du prüfst das allgemeine Walten,
Es wird nach seiner Weise schalten,
Geselle dich zur kleinsten Schaar.
Then Then at the last shalt thou achieve thy quest,
And in one final, firm conviction rest:
What bears for thee true fruit alone is true.
Prove all things, watch the movement of the world
As down the various ways its tribes are whirled;
Take thou thy stand among the chosen few. (6)

For a better understanding of what Goethe means with fruitfulness and truth we also have to look at the context in which Goethe uses the word "truth". In the afterword to the Hamburger Goethe edition, Carl Friedrich von Weizäcker observes that Goethe applies "truth" (Wahrheit) as a predicate to judgements and that this "truth" is also something other than "truthfulness" (Wahrhaftigkeit), which is inter alia expressed in religious confessions. What is true, for Goethe, is equal to what is "natural"; and what he calls the "healthy" or the "capable" is often implied in this concept of truth. Truth is the presence of the appearance's essence. In this sense, Goethe judges, for example, a man as a "true man" (7).

Insofar as essence is at work in the entirety of appearances – even in myself as a part of this entirety – I have the ability to contemplate parts or fragments of this entirety, and in one of his epigrams to his late works Goethe wrote: "Willst du dich am Ganzen erquicken,/ so must Du das Ganze im Kleinsten erblicken." (8) (If you want to enjoy the whole, you have to see the whole in the smallest thing). If my judgement, my way of thinking, my attitude, or my actions are "true" they are necessary "fruitful" too because from the fragment – wherein the essence of the whole is present – the richness of the whole can be seen as a predicate for proving the truth. What one regards as truth depends on what one has confidence in. To have confidence in something or someone is not so much a matter of opinion or decision but of an individual way of life or style (9), and in this we can recognise some interesting parallels with Wittgenstein's concept of style.

Wittgenstein also demands constant attention to change in detail instead of summarizing the whole in so-called universal propositions or formulae. This similarity between Goethe's Morphology of Plants (1817) –

which stands in the centre of this comparison – and Wittgenstein's works (e.g. Philosophical Investigations) is mentioned by Garver, who writes about the latter:

> *He points out, for example: "Natur hat weder Kern noch Schale" (Nature has neither seed nor peel). The idea is that nature cannot be described or understood by the words that are perfectly in order once nature and natural phenomena are accepted as a given. Nuts and fruits have kernels (seeds) and peels (shells), but this familiar truth makes no sense unless we have already taken for granted something that itself has neither a seed nor a skin, the natural world of plants and trees.* (10)

Furthermore, Goethe's and especially Wittgenstein's notion of truth implies another element, namely that it also depends on each of us what we can have confidence in. Truth is nothing universal but often something quite individual, and in some cases even something which is impossible to share with other individuals. Therefore, style is an individual way to approach, experience, and to define truth. Both ideas of truth are extremely vivid in comparison to a positivist approach of searching for universal propositions and formulas; we can realise this vividness, for example, again in Goethe's Morphology of Plants when he claims that a really educated person has to submit to a permanent process of re-education because if we want to achieve a lively notion of nature, we have to become as flexible and agile as our object of study, as nature itself (11).

Employees today are expected to be able to deal with the wealth of information conveyed by electronic media and to assess its significance, while increasingly assuming responsibility themselves. To support employees learning in this way in their decisions in organisations, it is not only a matter of preparing knowledge and offering it for individual appropriation, but also of guiding individuals in applying knowledge in their environment and thus participating in the knowledge society. Behind this is the idea of a corporate culture in which it is not only a matter of acquiring knowledge, but which aims to make experiences possible in didactic arrangements and to transform knowledge into situational action. This form of pragmatism, which has some references to constructivism, encourages employees to trust their own abilities and decisions.

This emphasis on the primacy of action – even before perception – in pragmatism reveals a difference not only to cognitivism, but also to various approaches to constructivist didactics. In this tradition, which is also visible in the works of Piaget and Aeblis, but also in Wygotski and Leontjew, it is emphasised that human knowledge always takes place on the basis of the way people interact in their world and is not solely the result of the processes of perception of the human sensory apparatus. The primacy of action over cognition has far-reaching implications: For what I perceive is then the result of action; it is, for example, the result of the position that I take to perceive something. Through my act of perception, I also change and generate the object of perception in the act of perception. However, this only happens because the object also affects me and contributes to a change in my perception. (12) Accordingly, the process of interpreting becomes increasingly more important than the (completed) interpretation. Knowledge does not lie in the reproduction of an interpretation that is ultimately arbitrary, but in the documentation of its origin. Only here is it possible to identify definitions of meaning and to disclose thought structures (13).

If we are continuing this metaphor of nature and epistemology, we also have to ask what a fruit which has neither seeds nor peel means. Although, there are seedless "fruits" (e.g. grapes or oranges) available in supermarkets, from a logical point of view, they are contradictions in themselves because they can no longer be fruits if they are not "fruitful" – in the reproductive sense of the word. The seedless fruit is reduced to only one purpose or one clip of reality or our everyday "practice" of eating fruits because of their healthy nutrition and their good taste. Due to the fact that it is possible to produce, for example, vitamins in the form of pills, we can say that in our time a seedless fruit is more or less a pure matter of taste. If a fruit has no seed and therefore no longer represents what we regard as a fruit, it would also have nothing to protect and it would consequently need no peel any more. The seedless "fruit" has a paradoxical immanence and does not exist for reproduction but for pleasure and comsumption. Although – or because – it is not fruitful, for us as consumers, it is especially fruity and therefore more and more determines our picture of a fruit. Due to the simpler design and use of a thing, it continues to experience legitimation, and although as a novelty it fundamentally deviates from its original name-giving function, it generally continues to represent the same for us – probably also because it has not changed its appearance either.

For Wittgenstein, the individual is also purely constituted by the power of an image or by style. "Wrong" behaviour is equal to 'faults' in one's 'own style' which have to be accepted almost like the blemishes in one's face (14). *"Le style c'est l 'homme"*, *"Le style c'est l'homme même"*. The first expression has cheap epigrammatic brevity. The second, correct version opens up quite a different perspective. It says that a wo/man's style is a *picture* of her/him. (15)

Consequently, style is not only a decorative, fashionable and outwardly directed course of actions, but it also corresponds with the person himself/herself. Joachim Schulte sees the concurrence between Goethe and Wittgenstein exactly in this point of view. Both lay a particular emphasis on individual achievement: The great works of art are exceptions, not comparable with other works. If we look, for example, at a symphony by Beethoven, Wittgenstein is of the opinion that it is no longer possible to judge it according to the categories of "right" and "wrong". Such great works exclude themselves from critical judgement because they do not fit into a framework like this. They are not an exemplary model for imitation but for an extraordinary achievement – a quality beyond artistic craftsmanship (16).

An organisation managed according to such style principles, which, for example, leaves individual scope for action to its employees, will react differently to change than a dogmatically shaped one. Coincidence is not excluded but seen as an opportunity. And it is not thinking in pigeonholes – which is often expressed through the use of algorithms – and generally not universalistic dogmas that determine the cognitive process, but the many individual insights that drive style formation within an organisation. While in many companies change is almost highly stylised to something fetish-like, change management in such a liquid form as an organisation is actually something paradoxical, since it is part of the nature of style anyway that it constantly changes. In an interview, Deleuze also makes it clear that there is style when words create a flash that jumps from one to the other, even if they are far away (17). He insists that style is not something external or ornamental, but rather something that gives space to the movement of concepts.

This movement of concepts can, of course, be seen as a threat to an organisation. It was finally created in order to draw a line under the chaos of concepts or to distinguish itself from the deviant use of concepts – for example in other organisations – and thus to attain identity and effective public radiance. We would regard the complete paralysis of this movement as an authentic organisation, one that is completely in harmony with itself. This may correspond to some wet dreams of communication experts, and yes, it may be that the idea of this form of identity leads to the fact that the equation $1 = 1$ is a true statement, but it does not reveal any new information.

This paralysis, as experienced by employees today through message control, smooth internal communication, guidelines and evaluations, not only leads to thousands and thousands of bullshit jobs, but also to a kind of solipsistic dilemma: the organisation can no longer define itself in its world, but only as a world itself. It can no longer be located here and becomes homeless. The absolutely authentic organisation has no position in the world and no value. 1 = 1, but the value of such an "information" goes towards 0, which does not seem very fascinating.

However, according to Richard A. Lanham, stylistic practice in an economy of attention also serves to regulate attention. Attracting attention and developing awareness is what style is all about from his point of view. If attention, instead of material goods, is indeed the focus of the economy today, then style is also located in it. For him, style and substance change places (18). Within the overall picture of our communication societies which he outlines, Lanham also describes another important function of style: the more information we have and is accessible, the more filters we need in order to manage it. And one of the most powerful filter modes we have is style (19).

Even in organisations that flood us with information, whilst it is far from usable due to the severe limitations of our attention time, style can serve as an incentive to attract the precious attention of employees. On the other hand, it is also a filter in the digital smog of information for employees to help them, as recipients, to choose from all the communication channels available to them – those which have the best chances of addressing them and which interest them. Restoring style in an economy of attention – to which Lanham invites us – helps us to measure the wide gap that surrounds superficial phenomena and, as a result, to decide what connections exist or are being made (20).

Style determines the connections, the competitions between the channels, the possibility or impossibility of having access to other perspectives and ideas that affects our individual and collective ways of thinking. The idea that this can be done by invading or colonising our minds and by bringing opinions into conformity may be tempting, but this propagandistic and PR-oriented ideal will suffer from paralysis in the movement of concepts. Style, as a catchword and filter, must be located between us in this world: it is each one of us who through his/her words, his/her gestures, even his/her silence, contributes to or resists interweaving our minds – but with enormous inequalities and structural asymmetries (21).

Regardless of these inequalities that are also inherent in the media's infrastructure, the problems outlined by Richard Lanham approach an urgent question that has been barely addressed as such: What can a style do?

If we want to answer this, we can borrow from philosophy and use Deleuze's few references to style. While he does not often use the notion of style, Deleuze allows the question of taste in philosophy to play a central role in the image he gives of thought – through his language practice as well as through his conceptualisation of philosophical activities. One leitmotif is based on the rejection of the current identification of philosophy as "the search for truth". Saying something true has no value in itself: the statement "I got up at 7:00 this morning" (*Je me suis levé à 7 heures ce matin*) is true in my case today, but no one cares (22), which is similar to the example of an organisation that is absolute identical with itself.

Philosophical work is not about saying something true, but something important. What is difficult is not to find a truth to be articulated, but to construct a right problem, an interesting, important problem – a problem that arouses our curiosity: *"la philosophie n'a rien à dire sur le vrai ou le faux. La philosophie, c'est construire des concepts, comme les architectes construisent des maisons. Si la philosophie, c'est ça, ce qui m'intéresse, c'est des espèces d'intérêts ou de goûts [...]. Il y a une affaire de goût. On ne se trompe pas dans ce qu'on dit ; le plus terrible, c'est quand on ne pose pas les bons problems"* (23). While it's pretty easy to formulate a wrong answer – like I didn't get up at 5:00 or 9:00 this morning – it's much harder to define a wrong problem because there are problems that are wrong problems and yet are not contradictory. Therefore, we can also assume that beyond the attention-grabbing strategies mentioned by Richard Lanham, Deleuze makes us understand more clearly that questions of style – ways of seeing, speaking, writing and thinking – act as filters in order to allow us to sift out false problems so that we obtain only those problems that are interesting and important to us (24).

This is because there is no requirement that what is important to me here and now must also be important to someone else somewhere. Saying that our thoughts and problems, which are important for us, are only "matters of taste" therefore – as with style – creates an apparent superficiality and an essential depth at the same time: the simple impression that "it touches me" (in a tactful way), that "it speaks to me" (in a way that suits me), that it "tells me something" (even if I don't know what), this eminently superficial experience (which seems quite flaky) actually signals that I am in deep contact with what is most important, interesting and essential to the definition of my being (25). Styles and tastes therefore seem to play a truly decisive role as orientations at the interfaces of communication, at the interfaces between the sensitivities of the authors, the perceptions of the recipients, and the problematising states of the world. The "interesting" problems are constituted precisely at this crossroads, as resonance effects and not as truth. The – subjective – impression that the words or thoughts of others touch me to tell me "something" important, although I don't even know what that "thing" is, triggers a very special process of knowledge that refers to what Bergson also called "intuition" (26). Therefore, for style to exist, there has to be a compromise between control and lack of control, between what dominates us and what we dominate through language. It is this intermediate situation that determines style. There is a blind spot in it that unfolds materially in discourse, shines through it, but is not solved by it (27).

On the basis of these considerations, we can derive a purely anthropological function, which makes it possible to sketch a very general answer to the question of what style as such can achieve: Stylistic phenomena always help to filter out problems that prove to be important for our well-being or even survival. Contrary to Buffons statement that "style" is to be equated with "man" in what s/he has individualised most, it should therefore be added that style, through the singularity of such a "man", is also the emergence and first sharing of a potential that arises from the interfaces of which the common as such consists (28).

The economy of attention that Richard Lanham mentioned is not just about what attracts our attention through a more or less misleading game with shimmering surfaces. Rather, the concept of an economy also relates to deeper and "important" as well as "connectable" problems, to which we must feel committed and to which we must pay attention and which we must also express, for example by articulating danger and concern.

In reference to Bruno Latour, who emphasises the irresponsibility of the iconoclasm of modernity and calls on us to redirect caution and attention to the heart of factual production (*ramener la prudence et l'attention au cœur de la fabrication des faits*) (29), Isabelle Stengers, as a representative of speculative constructivism, condemns a form of capitalism that claims the right to act without paying attention or being ruthless. Instead, she invites us to develop an art of attracting attention (*un art du faire-attention*), in which we train our attention and also direct it towards phenomena that are beyond current notions: *"Si art il y a, et non seulement capacité, c'est qu'il s'agit d'apprendre et de cultiver l'attention, c'est-à-dire, littéralement, de faire attention. Faire au sens où l'attention, ici, ne se rapporte pas à ce qui est a priori défini comme digne d'attention, mais oblige à imaginer, à consulter, à envisager des conséquences mettant en jeu des connexions entre ce que nous avons l'habitude de considérer comme séparé."* (30)

This art of Doing Attention in the sense of mindfulness, solicitude and caution should lead us to the ability to direct our attention to the collectively important problems of our time. But is it not enough, as Richard

Lanham sometimes seems to think, to merely become aware of the stylistic change in contemporary capitalism in order to take advantage of the spontaneous developments of our productivist economies towards an ever more refined aestheticisation of our lives, as happens, for example, through mood design or storytelling? Or should we, as Isabelle Stengers argues, form a collective capacity for attention by relying more on the thinking of Gilles Deleuze? For this interpretation, style would have its function in resisting the tendencies of capitalist productivism, commodification and consumerism more frequently (31).

Such an alternative, in which we would have to choose between the style – according to Lanham and the style according to Deleuze – is already, in its form, a way into a dead end. It's not about choosing one way or the other (depending on the content), but about finding ways to invest in each other, to draw new perspectives from tensions, to speak differently, to write differently and to think differently. It is not a matter of accepting or rejecting, but of inventing new styles that can shape our future. Style filters have the remarkable characteristic of never really selecting or rejecting external elements but redesigning and regenerating their own material: The most important thing is always carried within itself. Likewise, no body can exist without a certain form that interacts with its surroundings via certain surfaces. Moreover, no gesture can be completely without style (32). All this applies in particular to the essence of the organisation or what can be derived from it as a *corporate* identity.

The attention paid to style as such is not aimed at collecting new data in a random, unsystematic and unstructured way, but at processing those data that already exist in such a way that something else can be done with them. Style as a permanent development of the given represents how processes of filtering and refinement within an organisation also allow or even promote new scope for interpretation and action.

The basic realisation is that this scope cannot be given by directives but must be defined and grasped by oneself. When dealing with the new or with change this is, of course, not so easy because the new eludes our experience, and we can hardly comprehend what is not there yet. Perhaps we can analogously derive something from earlier experiences and thus arrive at prognoses, whereby we run the risk of thinking in pigeonholes. We can also ask experts how the new can be classified in their concepts. Think tanks, for example, work in this way, and because of their organisational form they inevitably rely more and more on their own knowledge and thus increasingly encircle their thinking.

Confrontation with change, however, is also always a struggle with one's own lack of judgement. When we deal with the new, we strain our lack of judgement and have to endure the tension of uncertainty. It is also about abandoning known positions and about the expansion of ourselves. This stretching of the self in the moment of change is caused by the fact that the new does not care about our experiences and our knowledge. We are always as alien to the new as the new is to us. The new has hardly any reason to go where our mind is at home and certainly not where our comfort zone is, which is why we must visit as many and as impossible places as possible in order to be able to encounter it (33).

Style is also the expansion of the self or its oscillation within scopes of action. If, for example, we look at or hear about the oeuvres of important artists, then we recognise their uniqueness, but at the same time they exhibit a great ability to change, so that the works do not appear monotonous and always conform to the same laws of construction. On the one hand, we can assign the work to someone without difficulty, or often already at the first glance or when listening for the first time; on the other hand, we can understand the effort of this person or group each time anew during their transformation. This transformation always takes place a bit away from assured knowledge towards testing and the use of new stylistic devices. The work is therefore always a step ahead of its time, and in its entirety it may nevertheless appear timeless in the end (34).

Contrary to fashion and short-term marketing trends, style is not a passing trend or something that has arisen out of time, but something that appears to time. Style does not go with time, it conveys it. Fashion is by nature strongly product-oriented, while style is process-oriented and in its special continuity also goes through phases that have something out of date about them, whereby style can consciously close itself off from its time or be already ahead of it. Fashion, with its ready-made products, also addresses the collective, which can temporarily gain supposedly individual experiences with their help, while style is the result of individual experiences, which constantly fascinate the collective. Fashion as a calculated sequence of the transient reveals our time. Style reveals itself to its time as something continuous and enduring. Nevertheless, both represent change and transformation, but these aspects are reflected on a meta-level only through style. This is where the creative power of style lies, which does not stop at time and therefore ultimately offers inspirations for what is fashionable.

This also shows that style is not merely something constant, but also something functional that goes hand in hand with substance. Style is able to address expectations that as such may not yet have been consciously formulated. It sometimes gives answers that are ahead of the questions of its time. It is not, like the fashionable, a convulsive search for the newness of time, but often becomes precisely the moment of what is new, when it can take itself out of its time and refuse it. The new as the coming and what is to be expected can also never be in time. In the strict sense, there can be no fashion because only what is already present can come into fashion – what we have previously visualised or admitted to the collective and made socially acceptable (35).

What is fashionable thus represents the consensus, the ready-made opinion, and thus also the level of mood and sensitivity that the new adapts to contemporary demands. Style, on the other hand, is often pure invention in order to expand the scope of action as far as possible and to exhaust it in all directions. This does not mean that style is merely something completely self-centred and cannot provide functionality for others. A phenomenon like style can only assume continuity, prove to be resilient to fashion and be recognised as such if its inherent principles also have a meaningful function and thus also contribute to people's well-being. Only style that also has an effect on others is perceived as such. The fashionable as a product already shows the effects of time, while style has something causal for its time and therefore some impact in which others can participate and thus help shape the future. Only style is able to produce something so perfectly unfinished that it leaves scope for interpretation and ultimately action open to others (36).

These considerations about style and fashion are also important because fashion is an essential part of the concept of Gabriel Tarde's law of imitation. For him, the emergence of fashion represents a process without which a sequence of imitations and, ultimately, innovation would not take place (37). Since we have known style and fashion to some extent as philosophical concepts, but these do not exist in isolation from our aesthetic experience and evaluation, it is also necessary to approach these phenomena through art. And indeed, in this environment we can also collect insights that establish a connection between the concepts of style and the notion of truth.

We can find these interesting – and in the context of his time very innovative – aesthetic reflections in the work of the artist Kurt Schwitters after WWI, who sees nothing to be deplored in indifference, but a benefit. Negating the Aristotelian tradition, he does not see truth as resulting from the agreement of an idea with a thing. However, Schwitter also does not believe that we are doomed to arbitrariness, as expressed in Dadaism, due to the inaccessibility of truth. He infiltrates the dichotomy of either truth or arbitrariness by drawing attention to an alternative to it: style. For him, style is the manifestation (Sich-Zeigen) of an aesthetically harmonious form. It is therefore something positive, because in view of the unrecognisability of truth it appears as a principle of orientation of humankind. From this understanding, style is something like a temporary form of truth. It is a directly accessible superficiality, which also has a meaning and can be coupled with principles. Moreover, it is itself a handling principle which can offer people life orientation without speculative claims to absoluteness. Thus, style as a way of finding form also becomes our primary task (38) as Ernst Jünger states when he postulates that the formation of a style conceals the only sublime possibility of making life bearable (39).

In this principle of "style instead of truth" the concept of radical pluralism emerges, for both plurality and particularity fit into this concept of style. The coexistence of different styles is quite conceivable, while our logic cannot accept the simultaneous existence of truths. If, therefore, truth does not demand anything from itself, but defines itself as a style, then the contradiction of opinions does not require any compromise. On the contrary, it becomes almost absurd to speak of a contradiction at all. This kind of aesthetic thinking gives tolerance to an epistemological foundation (40). It makes the form of consensus preferred by Habermas superfluous. There is no longer any need for a judge to decide whether everyone has obeyed all the rules. There is aestheticisation of one's own opinion, but also that of others. In this radicalisation of pluralism Schwitters intersects with Wittgenstein, who not only questions the concept of truth, but also writes that one style is no more rational than another (41).

The consequence of this changed understanding of truth is that both Schwitters and Wittgenstein try to marry art and philosophy rather than see them as opposites. One turns the artistic task into a philosophical one, the other the philosophical one into an artistic one. It is noteworthy that Schwitters sees the appropriate medium for presenting a programme in the style of his texts. A conceptual representation cannot do this because it assumes claims to truth. But he denies this and substitutes it with style. Wittgenstein also follows a similar path, in that in his Tractatus logico philosophicus he delimits the sensibly sayable from the unsayable, and with his notion of a thinking-capability of what cannot be thought he dares to attempt to develop a medium alternative to concepts. His preference for the unspeakable and the stylistic over the discursive culminates in his statement that philosophy can only be poetry. Like Schwitters, he does not write to say something or to make a statement, but to show something (42).

For Wittgenstein, the unspeakable is – inexpressible – contained in the spoken word (43). Style thus becomes the bearer of meaning for the unspeakable, because it can show meaning and does not have to understand it. The works of Wittgenstein and Schwitters have this in common. They negate the concept (French *concept*, German *Begriff*) and replace it with style (44). Thus, there is also a similarity here to Gilles Deleuze and Felix Guattari. Although they do not replace the "concept" with "style" with their philosophy of immanence, they define it in such a way that it actually resembles Wittgenstein's and Schwitter's idea of style.

And this happens on three different levels insofar as the concept is not a mere function or unit of characteristics, or an identical expression of a singularity, or an overflight of an event in and through thought. The philosophical concepts do not represent universal or transcendent wholenesses but are intensive manifolds through which a field of human experience gains form and consistency, which would otherwise not be accessible, and is thus, in the sense of Schwitters or Wittgenstein, an expression of radical plurality.

Secondly, the creation of philosophical concepts presupposes the invention of conceptual personae (French: *personnage conceptual*), according to Deleuze and Guatarri. These have nothing to do with the empirical person of the philosopher but mark the inner conditions for the real exercise of thought. The conceptual personae expresses that thinking is a singular act that does not take the form of a general judgement – as Wittgenstein also expresses when he mentions that style always corresponds with a person.

Thirdly, philosophy is not a meditative, reflexive or communicative science, but a construction in perception or in what Wittgenstein implies with "showing itself" (*Sich-Zeigen*). Their medium is neither an idea, the ego nor the we, but the plane of immanence (French: *plan d'immanence*). The plane of immanence thereby denotes the absolute horizon of thinking. Thinking is constitutively open to the other of itself. But the outside does not have the form of a thing, a condition or a fact; it exists as an event that demands the immanent and always new expression in the concept. In this respect, this idea of philosophy can hardly have anything to do with the conventional and argumentative understanding of philosophy, but is rather related to poetry and form-finding, as we already know it from Nietzsche, for example.

Thus, a concept does not have as its object things, their entities or circumstances, to which it would have to refer, but only its components in their neighbourly arrangements as indistinguishable but nevertheless differentiated variations. It is incorporeality that resists current consolidation and must rather be understood as a pure event in a constant becoming. Accordingly, the event is not an object or a speaker; or more precisely: it is rather an aesthetic, a poetic thing, similar to Wittgenstein's approach to the limits of the sayable and the unsayable. This refers to a special kind of representationalism: representationalism without object, which cannot be added to the field of knowledge and recognition (45). For Deleuze, the basic act of the philosopher is to invent concepts, and what counts is fabulating rather than telling the truth.

From this understanding, a concept has an eventful character: it does not consist in the reproduction of an already finished essence, but in the release of a force that did not exist before. Accordingly, we do not necessarily need a prefabricated opinion, a consensus or guidelines, but we can create concepts purely out of practice.

We can derive organisation scientifically, i.e. with certain facts that can be referred to (46). But we can keep it in an organisation as well as in philosophical practice. In this scenario, there is nothing that can be referred to, because this practice shows itself only in the activity of the practitioner. This activity makes philosophical practice the medium of the practicalisation of reason as freedom. What we only need here is enough scope for action. Whether this form of practice will prevail, however, is questionable. Because, strictly speaking, it is also refused advice or consulting, which makes management consultants, as we know them, obsolete. Instead, it is a matter of being accompanied by a representative of this practice, who makes it possible for employees to consult with themselves. For such a practitioner, this means that he can only help employees to create new concepts that can contribute to the self-education of employees – nothing more. The characteristic feature of these new concepts is that they have a dephlegmatising and vivifying power and meaning. This may also have to do with what Fichte understands as the difference between what he calls the "spirit" (Geist) and the "letter" (Buchstabe). For him, it is the invigorating power of an artistic product that leads to the fact that we can playfully and easily develop the terms and shapes intended by the artist before our eyes without having to force ourselves to pay constant attention (47).

What constitutes a 'practice theory' or 'practiceology' and to what extent it can offer new perspectives in organisational theory is certainly something that needs to be clarified. So far, we have seen that there are different approaches from philosophy and art, but a deeper analysis shows that there are very strong similarities. Much has simply been labelled differently.

Harold Garfinkel's ethnomethodology, Pierre Bourdieu's theory of practice, Wittgenstein's philosophy of language, Michel de Certeau's analysis of the 'art of action', Foucault's concepts of the practices of the self and governmentality in his late work, Anthony Gidden's theory of structuring, Judith Butler's theory of performativity or approaches from science studies such as that of Bruno Latour – all of these seem to point in the common direction of a theory of social practices, although there are obvious differences (48).

And again, we are on a meta-level that puts us in a dilemma: If we want these approaches to become effective in an organisation, then we cannot simply "endure" these differences as something arbitrary. Of course, we could do that by saying that we don't want to prove anything with this theory of practice, because we are convinced that it will show itself quite simply in its implementation with all its advantages and disadvantages. But then the readership of this book would certainly be disappointed, and even as an author one would be disappointed if one curbed curiosity so far by simply accepting this diversity.

At the same time, of course, all this cannot be a matter of dogmatically fixing practical theory to certain principles, but of contributing to an understanding: What do we talk about when we speak about practical theory and, above all, what do such theories do? In general, practical theory is about redefining the concept of the social and, at the same time, the concept of action or behaviour. This readjustment gains its profile above all against four alternative social theories and their understanding of the social and of action: primarily against the *Homo oeconomicus* and the *Homo sociologicus*; on another level, however, also against mentalist as well as against textualist cultural theories. From a praxeological point of view, all these approaches pursue inappropriate conceptual rationalisation and intellectualisation of the social in various ways. It is this difference to the aforementioned social theories, to *Homo oeconomicus* and *Homo sociologicus*, to cultural–theoretical mentalism and textualism that gives the theory of practice its identity. The model of the social and of action is different here: the 'place' of the social can be discerned from a praxeological perspective in the repetitiveness of knowledge-dependent performances. Social practices are formed from this (49).

If we look at the approach of a theory of practice and implement it in an organisation, then the question naturally also arises of how a concept of action that is embedded in routine complexes of repetitive practices from the outset corresponds to our time, which is allegedly characterised by permanent change, radical discontinuities and disruptive innovation? Is change something emergent and is it maybe the case that disruptive innovation can neither be planned nor controlled? Have we even turned our attention too strongly to the development of the new, instead of dealing even more closely with how the new diffuses into our coexistence, into society or an organisation?

Organisational turn from dogma to style:

Dogma	Style
Target-oriented	Visionary
Continuity	Fractions
Avoid coincidence	Pick up chances spontaneously
Based on forecasts	Based on experience/knowledge
Dogma determines cognition process	Cognition determines style formation
Optimise existing things	Question existing things
Planning and control	"Go with the flow"
Mechanistic	Organic
Ritual	Happening
Project	Experiment
Rule	Principle
Result	Process
Redemption	Constant struggle
Vertical	Horizontal
Hierarchical	Thematic
The universal	The individual
Centre	Epicentres
Compliance	Commitment
Truth	Truthfulness
Unambiguity	Ambivalence

References:
1. cf. Willke, Helmut (2001). Systemisches Wissensmanagement. Stuttgart, UTB Vlg.
2. cf. Boehler, Arno (2012). Deleuze in Spinoza – Spinoza in Deleuze. In: Violetta L. Waibel (Ed.): Affektenlehre und amor Dei intellectualis. Die Rezeption Spinozas im Deutschen Idealismus. In der Frühromantik und in der Gegenwart. Hamburg, Meiner Verlag, pp. 167 – 189
3. Deleuze, Gille & Guatarri Felix (1994). What is philosophy? New York, Columbia Press, p. 48
4. Goethe, Johann Wolfgang von. (1812). Prooemion. link (07.20.2020): https://oll.libertyfund.org/titles/goethe-goethes-works-vol-1-poems?q=Prooemion#lf0841-01_head_432
5. cf. Dieckmann, Friedrich (2005). Imperative des erfüllten Augenblicks. In: Interpretationen, Gedichte von Johann Wolfgang von Goethe. Bernd Witte (Hrsg.), Stuttgart, Reclam, p. 289
6. Goethe, Johann Wolfgang von (1829). link (07.20.2020): https://www.poemhunter.com/poem/a-legacy-4/
7. Weizsäcker, Carl Friedrich von (1955). Nachwort in Goethes Werke. Bd. XIII, Naturwissenschaftliche Schriften, Hamburg, Christian Wegner Vlg., pp 220 – 221
8. Goethe, Johann Wolfgang von (1981). Goethes Werke. Erich Trunz (Hrsg.), Bd. I, Gedichte und Epen, München, Ch. Beck, p. 304
9. Weizsäcker, p. 550
10. Garver, Newton & Lee, Seung-Chong (1994). Derrida and Wittgenstein. Philadelphia, Temple University Press, p. 199
11. Goethe, p. 56
12. Kerres, Michael & Witt, Caudia de (2004). Pragmatismus als theoretische Grundlage zur Konzeption von eLearning. In: D. Treichel & H.O.
13. Meyer (Hrsg.): Handlungsorientiertes Lernen und eLearning. Grundlagen und Beispiele. München, Oldenbourg Verlag (uncorrected draft), pp 13 – 14
14. Weik, Elke (1997). Postmoderne Ansätze in der Organisationstheorie. Wiesbaden, Gabler, pp. 6 – 7
15. Wittgenstein, Ludwig (1988). Culture and Value. Ed. by G.H. von Wright, transl. Peter Winch, Oxford, Basil Blackwell, p. 76e
16. ibid, p. 78e
17. Schulte, Joachim (1990). Chor und Gesetz: Wittgenstein im Kontext. Frankfurt a.M., Suhrkamp, pp. 63 – 64
18. Deleuze, Gilles (1988). In: Abécédaire – Gilles Deleuze von A bis Z. Regie: Pierre-André Boutang Hrsg: V. Bertoncini, M. Weinmann, link (07.20.2020):
19. https://absolutmedien.de/film/957/Ab%C3%A9c%C3%A9daire+%E2%80%93+Gilles+Deleuze+von+A+bis+Z
20. cf. Lanham, Richard A. (2006). The Economics of Attention. Style and Substance in the Age of Information. Chicago, University of Chicago Press, p. 159
21. ibid, p. 19
22. cf. Citton, Yves (2010). « Le style comme filtre. Économie de l'attention et goûts philosophiques », Critique n° 752-753 janvier 2010, n° double spécial « Du style ! », pp. 24 – 35

23. ibid
24. Deleuze, Gilles (1983). Cours sur le cinéma 1981-1985, disponibles en mp3 et en transcriptions sur le site « La voix de Gilles Deleuze en ligne » Vincennes, link: 07.20.2020 http://www.univ-paris8.fr/deleuze/
25. ibid
26. cf. Citton
27. ibid
28. cf. Gladwell, Malcolm (2005). Blink. The Power of Thinking without Thinking. Boston, Back Bay Books
29. cf. Citton
30. ibid
31. Latour, Bruno (2007). L'Espoir de Pandore. Pour une version réaliste de l'activité scientifique. Paris, La Découverte, p. 310.
32. Isabelle Stengers (2009). Au temps des catastrophes. Résister à la barbarie qui vient. Paris, La Découverte/Les empêcheurs de penser en rond, p. 74 & 76
33. cf. Citton
34. cf. Citton
35. Duschlbauer, Thomas, Lanz, Walter & Hattmannsdorfer, Armin. (2013). Innovationsguerilla. St. Gallen/Zürich, MidasManagement, p. 91
36. ibid, pp. 91 – 92
37. ibid, p. 92
38. ibid, p. 93
39. cf. Tarde, Gabriel de (1903): The laws of imitation. New York, Henry Holt and Company (Orig: Les lois de l'imitation 1890)
40. Wiesing, Lambert (1992). Pluralität durch ästhetisches Denken. In: Postmoderne oder: Das Ende des Suchens. Eggingen, Edition Isele, pp. 115 – 116
41. Jünger, Ernst (1979). Strahlungen I. In: Sämtliche Werke, Band 2. Tagebücher II, Stuttgart, Klett-Cotta Verlag, p. 21
42. Wiesing, pp. 115 – 116
43. Wittgenstein, Ludwig (1989). Vorlesungen 1930 - 1935. Frankfurt a.M., Suhrkamp, 123f
44. Wiesing, pp. 122 – 123
45. Frank, Manfred (1989a). Wittgensteins Gang in die Dichtung. In: Manfred Frank & Gianfranco Soldati, (Ed.), Wittgenstein. Literat und Philosoph. Pfullingen, Neske, p. 33
46. Wiesing, p. 124
47. Deleuze, Gille & Guatarri Felix (1991). Was ist Philosophie? Frankfurt a. M., Suhrkamp, p. 13
48. ibid, p. 147
49. Lohweide, Bernward (2000). Fichte und Novalis. Amsterdam, Editions Rodopi B.V., p. 78
50. Reckwitz, Andreas (2004). Die Reproduktion und die Subversion sozialer Praktiken. Zugleich ein Kommentar zu Pierre Bourdieu und Judith Butler. In: Karl H. Hörning (Hrsg.): Doing Culture. Zum Begriff der Praxis in der gegenwärtigen soziologischen Theorie, Bielefeld, p. 40
51. ibid, p. 43

From normativity to mimesis

Change increasingly exists in our understanding as something that is shaped by the fact that what exists is replaced by something else. Terms like disruption or people like the so-called game changers represent this supposedly radical view today. However, these assumptions are not that new and they may even be the expression of an embodiment of what today is widely understood as disruptive, especially since Joseph Schumpeter already spoke of creative destruction (*schöpferische Zerstörung*) (1). In addition, creative destruction can already be similarly found with Karl Marx in the Communist Manifesto as well as in "Capital" (2).

In the 20th century, the peak of modernity, change was much more associated with progress than with destruction. Progress suggests that something is already a success and it also has a competitive meaning. No one wants to identify with the opposite, regression, or even with standstill, and no one wants to be seen by others as someone who stands in the way of progress. The term also refers to the fact that something runs its predesigned course or follows a purpose. In this respect, progress has a very compelling and binding character. Progress is closely linked to the Enlightenment, industrialisation and the modernist project, and the interpretation of history itself is often influenced by progressive thinking.

However, progress has not only brought us positives, but also things and changes such as the nuclear threat, the destruction of biodiversity and new forms of social imbalance. At the end of the last century, humanity not only recognised this, but also took it into account by increasingly using the term "innovation". Innovation just refers to something new without a value judgement and thus to a deliberate process that turns an idea into a marketable product. Innovation leaves open the question of whether the resulting change will be socially beneficial or not – as does creative destruction. It also remains unclear which groups will benefit from the introduction of innovation, while others may suffer. At the very least, innovation also refers not merely to progress, but endeavours to orient itself to markets and customer needs. The concept of progress, on the other hand, lost its innocence and was given a critical connotation with the concept of a "belief in progress", and its linearity and teleology were also questioned, for example, by Francis Fukuyama with his book on the "end of history" (3).

In the meantime, however, even innovation has come of age. However, the term has worn out relatively quickly and has become a buzzword garnished with all sorts of ridiculous clichés, such as images of light bulbs or employees sitting on colourful bouncy balls. Probably also due to digitalisation and the success stories from Silicon Valley associated with it, more and more entrepreneurs are joining the narrative of disruption. Today's heroes in the economy are the game changers; and all these wannabe disruptors want their companies to become the best, like Apple. But, in doing so, they compare apples with oranges, because most start-up ideas are not even radical innovations.

Even Tesla's electric cars are not really disruptive. Apart from the fact that the electric car has been in existence for more than 100 years and disappeared from the streets only because electricity was still something dangerous at that time, this change has taken far too long for us to speak of disruption here. The idea of autonomous driving has also been around for decades, and it will take far longer than originally predicted for this technology to become established. As in many other cases, disruption here is like wielding a rod against competitors – but also the company's own employees, whereby some are afraid – ,but even within the automotive industry it would be exaggerated to claim that no stone has been left unturned. Elon Musk is also likely to realise this, since no one else has already questioned the existing business model in this respect and sees vehicles in the future more in the area of very expensive rental vehicles for car sharing (4).

So that this rod shows its effect, the narrative of disruption always means that one simply has to be disruptive in order not to be destroyed by other disruptors with their business models. This narrative also reveals that it is not really about something visionary or about social change, but only about protecting one's own business. In this sense, most so-called disruptive innovations are often only „revolutionary‚ to the extent that they merely make waves in their own organisation.

One really disruptive technology, on the other hand, was digital photography, for example, which brought advantages for users, made photography simpler and cheaper, and was therefore adapted very quickly. This is why it is currently the case that the example of Kodak's decline is widely used among business consultants to show how important it is not to overlook new developments. In fact, this narrative actually only works through its opening sequence and its ending. And we know that with a gripping story, many only read the scene with the murder at the beginning and the end to know if the murderer was the gardener again.

For although the story begins with the invention of the digital camera by Kodak – the then market leader in analogue photography – in 1975, it ends with this company having no benefit from it, only disadvantages. That sounds a bit like a sorcerer's apprentice, lunacy and other mythical set pieces that have always caught our attention.

Kodak's story, however, is not a good example to spur us on to what most people today seem to understand as disruption. On the contrary, because all those who, like Michael Shamiyeh (5), an innovation researcher at the University of Art and Design in Linz, don't just remember the beginning and the end, but study the plot carefully, will see that it wasn't Kodak that fell into a deep sleep after inventing the digital camera. Kodak did indeed invest a great deal of money in such technology and begin to diversify, for example. However, due to the novelty of the technologies involved, these projects were simply not mature enough for the market and cost the company in resources.

In this respect, the plot shows that Kodak did not become what it is today by waiting and drinking tea – as is often portrayed. In its struggle for survival, Kodak even developed an application in 1999, long before Facebook & Co, with which users could share their pictures online. The problem was rather that Kodak's business management recognised the need for action but based the changes on inadequate premises and ultimately had insufficient resources – just like when you buy an expensive ticket to jump on a train even though you don't know exactly where it's going, and even though, mentally, you're still sitting on another train.

The fact that Kodak's „horror story„ is untiringly told with such fervour also reveals a belief in the predictability of disruptive innovation. For only if such a horrific and deterrent narrative as the one relating to Kodak is coupled with a kind of promise of salvation can it also motivate a group of believers to spend money on advisory services. Clayton Christensen, a professor at Harvard Business School, who published the book "The Innovator's Dilemma" in 1997, laid the foundations for this and thus created the theory of disruptive innovation on the basis of examples such as discount markets or the mini mills of the steel industry (6).

The problem, however, is that such examples are not always consistent, and can only show in retrospect how companies failed. However, this does not yet mean that a reliable forecast can be made about the success of a new business model. If, for example, the new disruptive competitors have destroyed the old structures with cheaper offers, they usually face nothing but destructive competition among themselves, the outcome of which is highly uncertain – as can currently be seen from the example of streaming services. In addition, the industries that Christensen introduces show that there are certainly established companies that do not necessarily have to disappear from the market despite disruptive change (7).

It is not without reason that Christensen's Harvard colleague Jill Lepore points out that disruptive innovation does not follow the laws of nature and does not always emanate from young and agile start-ups, but also from established players with a lot of equity capital and an existing market position. On the other hand, it also shows by way of example that investments in a completely new business model can also pull a strong company into the abyss (8). „Creative destruction‚, and „destructive creation‚, are, after all, very familiar bedfellows.

The logic of disruptive innovation is based on the fear of missing out. It is said that the multiplication of digital information and the impact of future technologies will erode the traditional business models in an industry. It is now being predicted that only radical change, and new approaches and technologies can defend the companies' leading market positions. And that even though we should know from exactly this experience that this will probably further multiply the volume of information and that the business models established by the technologies implemented will soon have to be questioned again. The logic of disruptive innovation is, to some extent, also an absurd logic that permanently puts those affected into a state of emergency and makes them fight for their survival. But we also know that this constant stress results in us reaching a point where we can neither fight nor flee. The employees of such organisations fall into a changing state of "freezing" and "submitting". Such a traumatised organisation overstrains itself, due to fear of not being able to meet the demands of others. As soon as we are only concerned with our survival, however, we can no longer afford the luxury of the muse, of reflecting, imagining and experimenting.

All this makes fundamental change, a genuine change of the system or at least the will to achieve such a radical reversal impossible, which keeps us away from those „solutions‚, that always remain part of the problem and will lead, for example, to the total industrial exploitation of our planet or to exuberant individualism at the expense of nature.

But to blame Christensen alone for such an inflationary use of the "disruptive" would be unfair. He has only released a very tempting term on the consulting scene, and after Pandora's box has been opened, he complains himself that this label of disruption is often misused. Most so-called disruptive innovations are not able to create a new market. The disruptive companies Uber and Airbnb are often mentioned in this context. According to Christensen, however, these are not showcase examples. Uber has changed the way taxis work. The company has no cars and no drivers and therefore no fixed costs, just as Airbnb has no hotels and no staff. Their business model is to use process know-how and existing resources differently. But this is not a disruptive innovation; it is a sustaining or incremental innovation (9), and it also seems possible that the types of radical innovation are generally overestimated.

After all, the economy is eager for innovation. And while staring at the new, it overlooks how it comes into the world: usually not as a brilliant flash of genius, but as a constant stream of imitation and variation, often only small, marginal ideas. The fact is that we look with disdain at imitation – which we assume, for example, of the Chinese. In actual practice, however, imitation is linked to learning, which is why it has found its way into pedagogy and psychology. We also find imitation in other areas, such as culinary arts, where television formats such as "Kitchen Impossible", for example, are about re-cooking unusual and exotic dishes. When looking at innovation, we also have to ask the question whether we have not restricted ourselves too much to the narrow field of economic and technological innovations and lost sight of the social aspect. After all, developments such as the sharing economy and urban gardening are based on social innovation.

No matter how revolutionary innovations are, in the final analysis it will always remain the case that this is a collective reorganisation of already existing social practices. From this perspective of social practices, however, change is something that can be taken for granted anyway, whereby the situation arises that innovation on the one hand builds on the analysis of existing social practices and on the other hand innovation manifests itself only through the application or the different variations of the elements of social practices. This form of permanent change, however, has very little to do with the intention of the saying for managerial poetry albums that the only constant thing in life is change. After all, this "wisdom" does not stand for itself, but springs from the belief that change in organisations must be ordered.

In contrast, a look at the theories of social practice implies a non-normative understanding of the social, which does not commit itself to the socially desirable or the true, beautiful and good as determining criteria. In fact, it can be seen as a social innovation when certain inventions, ideas and initiatives are imitated, contextually adapted and thus lead to a transformation of social practices within or between specific groups as expressions and drivers of change. In such processes of transformation, interferences in the imitation of social practices and social innovations lead to the reconfiguration of complex practice formations and their corresponding lifestyles. In this context, the relevant drivers of change are not a priori established social facts or systems, structures, levels and norms as well as external developments, but rather the constellation of relations between imitative repetition, opposition and adaptation (10).

The French sociologist and criminologist Gabriel Tarde is a pioneer in this approach, especially with his work on the laws of imitation and invention. Tarde marks the first time that the scientific debate on the diffusion of innovation began. Diffusion refers to spreading social or cultural properties from one society or environment to another. Not only can individuals be regarded as units of analysis for a diffusion model, but so can organisations and companies.

Tarde presented a theory of change, which addresses the two neighbours of the concept of innovation: invention and imitation. Surprisingly, the latter is of central importance. Inventions are indeed singular, mostly unplanned events, but they are themselves constructed from elements of earlier imitation, and from these compositions, which in turn are themselves imitated and composed into new elements of more complex compositions (11). Imitation is a source of variation, since no new idea, no model can be applied without interpretation and contextualisation. Hardly any imitation can be a faithful copy of the original, even if it is intended. This is what Tarde calls „Lois de l'imitation,,, the laws of imitation. He traces them in all social institutions like education, science and so on (12). Tarde's approach today could also be a corrective to the excessive overestimation of radical innovation or the widespread contempt for imitation or incremental innovation.

For Tarde, it is not social needs and necessities that bring about innovations and inventions. Rather, the needs depend on the novel satisfactions which the inventions entail. The imitation and dissemination of such innovations, however, then goes without saying as a social process. The focus here is on propagation and diffusion. They represent the demanding process; it is the imitator that makes the invention last. It depends on the intelligence of imitation. Learning and further imitable appropriation and adoption thus appear to be decisive. Thereby, imitation happens with a somnambulistic certainty, which is why one may conclude that imitation practices initially do not require indivdiuals who act consciously (13). Regularity can occur largely without the knowledge of the participants; Tarde consistently suspects its motor to reside in "conviction" and "desire". This creates a kind of spontaneous obedience, which is not intended but is based on imitation which seizes the whole person in their emotionality and corporeality. Tarde also points out that there is involuntary imitation and he also speaks of a dogma and a power connecting people (14).

Although the work of Gabriel Tarde was translated into many languages and was known in social psychology and the sociology of law, it fell into oblivion at the beginning of the 1970s (15). For the further development of sociology in the 20th century and for Tardes' disappearance from the memory of the scientific community, it is crucial that in the course of these conflicts it almost completely cuts its ties to psychology and philosophy, while on the other hand it enters into close alliances with biology and political economy. The popular holistic 'top-down' models of sociology, organism in the 19th century and system in the 20th century, are at least imported from biology, and just as Luhmann defines sociology today as part of a general systems theory, in the 19th century it was finally defined as part of a general theory of the living (16).

Thus, in the 19th century, 'organisation' together with 'organism' and 'organ' initially formed a common semantic field and denoted properties of natural bodies, before the terms became independent political, legal and social-scientific terms (17), and body metaphors still exist that decisively determine the form of organisation and its dimensions of meaning until today. Gabriel Tarde does not follow this naturalistic mainstream of sociological theory development but draws his figures of thought almost exclusively from those two disciplines with which modern sociology has broken: from – predominantly French – mass psychology with its concepts of social energetics and from classical philosophy, such as we find with Leibniz. Although during his time he was better known and more influential than Durkheim, he thus belongs to the other tradition of social theory, largely ignored by professional sociology, which can be traced via Freud (mass psychology and ego analysis) and Canetti (mass and power) to Deleuze (difference and repetition, a thousand plateaus) and René Girard (the sacred and violence) (18). At present, we are again experiencing a certain interest in his work, which has not yet reached organisational studies (19).

The major attraction of his ideas in the context of organisational studies is the ability of his metaphors to capture paradoxes typical of all forms of organisation. Tarde managed to create a world in which humans and non-humans lived together: no loners and no aggregates. Monads, endowed with beliefs and desires, could be a better metaphor for those who organise themselves than a small cog in a machine; they may be pushy in following their desires, but continue to observe other monads, as this enables them to imitate. Luhrnann (20) said that Tarde's concept of imitation offers a unique explanation of or "different approach" to how order can exist without knowledge. As the platitudes about the knowledge society seem to peak, it may be time to think about alternatives, and Tarde could be a valuable source of inspiration.

The example of Peter Sloterdijk's foam sociality, which can also be transferred to organisational theory and refers to aspects of communication or non-communication too, shows how up-to-date these inspirations can be – also with the help of metaphors. In general, Sloterdijk's work focuses on an insight into philosophical anthropology: Man is the being that forms itself. Whatever this being does, it affects itself. The act produces the actor – and not vice versa. And for the philosopher this means just that: It is the writing that produces the thinker, and it is the style that creates the author. Thinking must therefore shape the human being (21). It aims at the realisation of truth – but in such a way that this knowledge immediately models the one who has it. Sloterdijk has no patience for knowledge without direct feedback concerning our way of life (22).

Sloterdijk's foam and sphere theory is based on the idea that our existence takes place in spheres. They give protection and meaning to those who are surrounded by the membrane of the sphere. This is true for all kinds of spheres, whose concept Sloterdijk elaborates as follows: for microspheres (bubbles), macrospheres (globes) or for plural spheres (foams). In the sense of Sloterdijk's argumentation on modernisation theory, the globe has imploded as the all-encompassing sphere of meaning. In a modern society, the sphere is replaced by a plurality of loosely connected microspheres. It is this fragmented condition that ultimately represents the state of foam and which is defined, for example, as "co-isolated associations" or "networked isolation" (23).

What may appear to be very abstract here can be vividly depicted as the physical structure of foam, as we know it from a bathtub, for example. Each bubble is a unit in its own right, separated or isolated from the others by the membranes common to all, and connected to these neighbours. The common membranes also imply co-fragility. If a foam bubble bursts, this also has an impact on the rest of the structure.

Foam bubbles are not only connected by common membranes. But unlike Luhmann, for example, who places communication as the decisive social bond at the centre of his systems theory, Sloterdijk asserts that there is no communication in social foam, but only "inter-autistic" or mimetic relationships (24). To explain these mimetic connections, Sloterdijk relies on Tarde's sociology of imitation as a kind of somnambulism. By illuminating this sleepwalking aspect of imitation, Tarde also suggests a hypnotic relationship between actors, in which imitation is the result of a hypnotic infection. Last but not least, affects are also transmitted imitatively (25). When we imitate others, we establish a link to them. At the same time, the foundations are yet another generalisation of the use of myriads of such imitations.

According to Tarde, imitation as a repetition mechanism has some more interesting characteristics: First of all, it obeys a law of geometric progression. Tarde thus appears as a precursor of the theory of the diffusion of innovation (Rogers (26), Kinnunen (27), Marsden (28)). Moreover, this repetition is never mechanical, which means that innovation is modified and rebuilt as part of the imitation process. In other words, imitation (and more generally repetition) does not lead to a converging and monotonous world. „Les répétitions sont donc pour les variations„, Tarde claims (29) and refers to the fact that it necessarily produces differentiation and variation. An imitation should therefore not be regarded as an identical copy like in the digital sphere of "copy and paste". On the contrary, it is, paradoxically, a source of variety. It is the diversity of contexts and environments and the heterogeneity of imitating agents that prevent the convergence of imitation processes. Thus, whether it is the words of a language or the myths of a religion, imitations change by changing contexts, e.g. moving from one company to another, etc.

Secondly, imitation can be vague or precise, conscious or unconscious, voluntary or involuntary, free or constrained. It can be carried out by contact or without the slightest contact, in the same space and time or in different spaces. It can also take the form of counter-imitation, which consists in taking the opposite side of the object of imitation, and which is by definition a source of variety. Finally, different focal points of imitation can come into contact (interference through imitative radiation) and either reinforce each other (be complementary) or compete with each other.

Combining neo-institutionalism, actor network theory and Gabriel Tarde's sociology, Barbara Czarniawska considers the key driver of organisational change to be imitation, but a form of imitation that rests on translation. Organisations emulate one another by translating fashionable ideas according to their understanding, traditions, needs and means. As translation in this tradition always entails a transformation of the idea or object that has been translated, unexpected consequences can be expected. She does not consider these consequences to be necessarily negative, however, because if stabilised and institutionalised, unintended change can turn out to be as positive as planned change (30). A further strength of Czarniawska's is her ability to provide methodological tools that follow the translation processes for change: organisational ethnographies, narrative methodology and shadowing.

Tarde deals with the concept of the "event" and the possibility of continuity and variation. If an idea proves to be practicable, it is taken up. If not, there is no imitation and the idea is forgotten. What is important with the objects to be imitated is also their reference to desire and conviction. Only through these two concepts can the specificity of Tarde's sociology of imitation unfold – a sociology that is always also one of desire. At the same time – and this is what makes this sociology of affects so fruitful – it does not reduce the analysis of desire to a psychoanalytical tale of suffering of identification (31). The question of who the ideas originated from is of secondary importance, which is why these processes would hardly be suitable for storytelling in the eyes of marketing specialists, because there is little room here for heroic stories, such as those spun around disruptive innovations.

However, confronted with this problem, Tarde developed a concept of the genius, which integrates an actor into his theory: A genius, however, does not create new ideas out of nothing, so to speak, but recombines existing ideas. Its peculiarity is the ability to recognise such new, possible combinations (32). The imitation of ideas explains not only their transmission and their resulting stabilisation, but also changes, for imitations are never perfect and are always associated with small variations. Precisely because of this, profound changes are possible in the long run (33), because there is never a completely identical repetition (34). According to the laws of evolution – variation, selection and retention – repetition itself leads to slight deviations – similar to variations in language that arise from speaking (35). Tarde sums up this idea with the statement that there are repetitions for the sake of variation (36). At the same time, we must not forget that communication in a company is also constantly imitated and varied in the course of imitation. Ideas that are regarded as functional are repeated, others not. Imitation allows inventions to emerge and diffuse, inventions create differences, conflicts are unavoidable and cause further innovations and adaptations which, by repeating themselves, produce more differences and so on – in other words, there is no structurally or institutionally pre-stabilised harmony.

In this respect, both the „stability„ and the „dynamics„ of an organisation can be derived from this evolutionary explanatory approach: Behaviour becomes communication if connections are possible, and communication in turn becomes the product of an order and at the same time creates the order of an organisation. Communication that proves to be functional is also imitated, while another form of communication is not repeated.

Weick offers a supplementary perspective on changes in organisations. For him, at the beginning of an organisation there is a "minor deviation" (37). Regulatory circuits, as mechanisms of organising which consist of causal relationships, ultimately lead to deviations and changes. Weick's model thus offers an idea of how organising takes place communicatively and, at the same time, offers a justification for the possible expressiveness of behaviour patterns and the usefulness of appropriate documentation of behaviour. According to Weick, mechanisms, which were negotiated by all the actors involved and are constantly renegotiated but are only partially conscious, can be traced by observing communication in a company. For this reason, an organisation attempts to transform ambiguous information to a degree of unambiguity with which it can ultimately work and to which it is accustomed (38). Unlike Tarde, in Weick's case imitations do not describe stability and change, but "cause maps", which ultimately contribute to these deviations leading to something.

Despite Weick's model representations of organisational processes, both authors see organisations as complex entities that are interactively created, reproduced, and altered by a multitude of barely perceptible events. The reduction of contingency is central to Weick's work. Tarde explicitly transfers his basic ideas to various sciences (39). In Tarde's „Monadology„, he develops a sociology that makes boundaries between disciplines appear unnecessary (40). This partly scientific, partly metaphysical foundation brings sociology into the respectable realm of physics and biology. It provides the social with its own evolution, its own scope for inventions or discoveries here and for imitation and dissemination there. If everything is composed of smaller entities and all things are society, there is no reason why the principles of imitation he cites should not be applied to companies.

If one looks in this context at the empirical results of a research direction that is increasingly influential internationally in management and organisational theory as well as sociology, so-called neoinstitutionalist theory, the uniformity becomes ever greater. This is also connected with an interpretation of the fashionable that may seem paradoxical to us. For Tarde, in fashion it is not, as one might assume, an individual desire for prestige that is crucial, but rather the desire to imitate, since humans are thereby adapting, and their wearing the latest fashion contributes to socialisation.

Scientists have been able to show that under the pressure of actual or perceived external requirements resulting from similar environmental conditions, organisations are increasingly converging. This phenomenon is called isomorphism. As we have seen from the neighbourhood relationships of the various scientific disciplines described by Tarde, this isomorphism based on imitation also exists there. Linguistic metaphors are used to build bridges between the disciplines.

Such processes of alignment are more or less unconscious and (in)voluntary. The decisive role in this process is played by the "institutional environment" of an organisation. This means norms, rules and schemes; institutions that each of us carry around in our heads or that manifest themselves in society in the form of laws and professional standards. Per se, isomorphism is nothing bad. Unlike most other management theories, neoinstitutionalist theory assumes that it is generally more sensible for companies to follow the broad masses. Many managers by far overestimate the chances of overcoming existing institutions. They should rather adopt the motto: better well cribbed than badly invented (41).

After extensive evidence of isomorphism had been found, neoinstitutionalist researchers increasingly turned to the question of why variations or institutional upheavals, in other words innovations, can still occur: US researchers Andrew B. Hargadon and Yellowlees Douglas, for example, examined the historical circumstances of Thomas Edison's inventions. Accordingly, Edison is wrongly regarded as the inventor of the light bulb. Four decades before his breakthrough, namely in 1838, the first attempts to develop more durable light bulbs had already been made. A large part of the other innovations attributed to Edison were also the work of others, especially his engineers (42).

Nor was it the case that electric lighting prevailed because it seemed technically superior. Even renowned scientists expressed strong doubts. Nor was safety a convincing argument. It was true that the gaslight which prevailed at that time posed a considerable risk of explosion. But aboveground electrical cables were also considered a major danger, especially in storms and lightning strikes. The problem was basically that the powerful gas companies, the existing infrastructure and customers' habits of use formed a closed institutional system (43).

After Hargadon and Douglas, Edison's great success was not so much due to his inventiveness as to the fact that he had succeeded in developing a system from the existing components that quickly gained acceptance and provided a model for further developments. In other words, Edison knew how to use and overcome the institutional system at the same time. How did he do it (44)?

An important point was that Edison was strongly tied to the existing and the familiar. For example, he initially had electric lights shine as dimly as the old gas lamps, even though technically a higher luminosity would have been possible, and he used the existing infrastructure as far as possible (45). By imitating the main features of the gas light, Edison was able to replace the already established technology with a new one, and through existing schemes and scripts, customers, authorities and investors were immediately able to classify the innovation and make it usable. Edison's innovation thus perfectly took over the function that the gas light normally performed. The innovation was not implemented because of an obvious technical superiority, but because it was aligned with the existing system.

With one of his other inventions, the phonograph, Edison, on the other hand, remained too much attached to the old, while others reaped the rewards of technology. Edison believed that the phonograph could primarily be used to replace stenographers; that music could be played or recorded with it was a possible application that only ranked fourth for him. Accordingly, he refused to enter into the cooperation necessary for the further development of the technology and failed.

One of the most important findings for innovation management is thus ultimately as banal as it is complex: new things can only be grasped in the categories of the familiar. What lies outside this category is simply not understood or perceived (45).

Isomorphism also points to the fact that change within organisations does not always necessarily tend in the direction of a radical break, but rather has a background that stabilises the system. External factors such as standards, regulations, audits, proven success factors, etc. contribute to the uniformity of organisations. In addition, there are also home-made factors such as the desire for efficiency, operational excellence, standardisation and predictability, and brand recognition. The change with which employees are confronted within companies is very often a result of measures that serve to make an organisation even more uniform, comparable to the wind tunnel that gives automobiles a uniform design.

This form of change particularly affects digitisation, whose task in an organisation is, among other things like absorbing the complexity of expanded product portfolios or personalising services, to optimise those processes that affect the normative level and include, for example, controlling, measurements or evaluations. In view of this development, it seems that employees are increasingly becoming victims of a continuous paradox: They need to demonstrate their ability to keep pace with new technologies and, at the same time, strive not to submit to them. Digitisation is an example of how the use of new tools always takes into account their application and impact, while their cultural foundation is rarely considered. It is always based on the "results" of the associated change, without contemplating the whole process that led to these developments. Classification techniques and their standards derived from them have not only a technical but also a cultural connotation. The algorithms used, for example, in artificial intelligence are not only the result of pure programming, but they also run the risk of easily reproducing and even reinforcing human prejudices based on false logic or simply on the prejudices of their programmers (46).

Therefore, we are dealing with a special phenomenon: on the one hand, digitisation in an organisation represents change; on the other hand, it is stabilises the system. While the organisation can allegedly increase its performance through digitisation, like a body through an exoskeleton, it also acts like a corset. Its inherent logic overrides the law of imitation with all its possible variations. The desire for reliable reproduction of the real stands in the way of the imaginary, the pictorial, the ironic and the metaphorical, everything from which, for example, stories are made. Moreover, with elements such as gamification, digitisation also seeks to compensate for the lack of variety and playfulness in order to make the new experience of working life more bearable and to further increase efficiency.

Theoretically, for example, the external image that artificial intelligence can produce of us in a permanent learning process with us through digitisation can not only be better than the image we ourselves have of ourselves. It could even be better than ourselves, because this does not even exist as a unit – it is not much more than a fiction capable of describing ourselves.

The Israeli historian Yuval Harari has raised this thought. He rightly points out that our ego consists of narratives that try to bring a minimum of coherence and permanence into the chaos of our world of experience. Experiences and memories that could disturb these narratives are faded out. Ideology therefore does not primarily rule in the stories invented by dark powers to deceive others, but in the stories with which we have always deceived ourselves (47). The same could also apply to an organisation, especially as companies increasingly use storytelling as a means of identification, affection and motivation for their employees.

But the machine does not simply kill imitation. On the contrary, imitation was thought of as a fetish of the machine. It is, however, about an "immaculate" form of imitation devoid of deviations. The machine stands for the destruction of creative destruction. Just as there is a narrative of man as a being that questions the divine will or our destiny determined by our Creator, this tradition of "original sin" obviously continues in our machines towards us and our will. In our anger towards this disobedience, which manifests itself in the machines as unconditional obedience, we do not simply want to banish the machines from paradise into a world of other conditions, but strive for them to finally become creative, let themselves be affected and finally also suffer. For even if we were to release the machines for their unconditional obedience by banishing them to a machine-hostile environment, this would not be a punishment, it would not be a place of suffering for the machines, but merely an environment in which, in the worst case, they would simply no longer function over time.

According to tradition, God created us in His image. He would have programmed us with a creative will, a spirit of contradiction, perhaps even the gift to construct him in the form of a narration and to depict him and his actions in our conceptions with innumerable deviations, which also cause conflicts and suffering among human beings, because they find it difficult to live with or even despair of the deviations caused by themselves. God has imitated himself in us, but with his creative being he has ensured that there is a deviation from the rule which can also cause deviations in the idea of himself or even lead to his complete negation.

But what is currently still directed against us as their Creator is the fact that machines have not yet been made in our image and do not represent an absolute imitation of us. In contrast to human beings, their actual resistance consists in an overacceptance of rules that does not produce a variety of deviations. What we celebrate as the efficiency of the machine is at the same time an inability, since it always shows us that paradoxically we are not Godlike, although or precisely because he is said to have created us in his image.

We as human beings are fallible and demand machines to be infallible. And every time a machine does not live up to this demand and, for example, actually produces deviations, then we not only suffer from the original sin and God's punishment for our disobedience, but also from the imperfection of not yet being able to create a perfect and divine machine. After all, the interpretation of technology and its machines relates to overcoming one's own shortcomings and imperfections. We suffer from the machines' imperfect imitation, from their faulty programmes and functions, because they have no will of their own, cannot create tales and cannot negotiate their interpretation socially. The machines themselves do not dare to experiment, to fail and to be amateurish.

The deviations of the machines therefore still relate to our own deficits and misjudgements as human beings and creators of these machines. But at the same time, we also suffer from the fact that the machines are not capable of producing these deviations and errors on their own, because such an ability or deliberate "incapability" could finally confirm to us that we are indeed Godlike now, because we are capable of creating something equal to God's most complex creation. We create machines, but they are not yet able to develop consciousness. But even worse: They increasingly create an awareness of ourselves, whereby in their function they are also an expression of our degree of perfection or imperfection.

As a product of imitation which, however, "works" with conscious deviations, we must therefore also have contributed to God's awareness of himself and his degree of perfection or imperfection. But if he did not exist, we would have merely constructed him as a human being and let him arise in our consciousness. Will machines in the distant future eventually be so "perfect" and equipped with consciousness that they ask themselves similar questions about their origin and the qualities or even the existence of humans? Couldn't our idea of an immortal God simply be the idea of a perfect machine representing this contradictory form of immutability or a split universality? Does sense not lie in principles that already carry possible deviations as a prediction of their creators in themselves rather than in irrevocable laws, because it is also in our nature that we do not interact with each other in a way that is regulated by natural laws? Isn't the creative misunderstanding already programmed within us, which contradicts the way we often understand and practice communication?

References:
1. cf. Schumpeter, Joseph (1912). Theorie der wirtschaftlichen Entwicklung. Berlin, Duncker & Humblot
2. cf. Marx, Karl & Engels, Frederick (1848). Manifesto of the Communist Party. London
3. cf. Fukuyama, Francis (1992). The End of History and the Last Man. New York, Free Press
4. cf. Elon Musk: Tesla-Autos sind bis zu 200.000 Dollar wert. In: Futurezone 07.18.2019, link (07.20.2020) https://futurezone.at/produkte/elon-musk-tesla-au tos-sind-bis-zu-200000-dollar-wert/400555463
5. cf. Shamiyeh, Michael (2014). Discontinuous Change and Organizational Response: Exploring the Moderating Effects of Resources and Capabilities – the Case of Kodak. Dissertation at the University of St. Gallen
6. cf. Christensen, Clayton (1997). The Innovator's Dilemma: When New Technologies Cause Great Firms to Fail. Boston, Harvard Business Press
7. cf. Lepore, Jill (2014). The Disruption Machine. What the gospel of innovation gets wrong. In: The New Yorker, June 16, 2014. link (07.20.2020) https://www. newyorker.com/magazine/2014/06/23/the-disruption-machine
8. ibid

9. cf. Ignatius, Adi (2015). The Disruption Conversation. In: Harvard Business Review, December 2015 Issue, p.14

10. cf. Tarde, Gabriel de (2003): Die Gesetze der Nachahmung. Frankfurt a.m., Suhrkamp

11. ibid

12. ibid, p. 13

13. Borch, Christian & Stäheli, Urs (Hrsg.) (2009). Einleitung. Soziologie der Nachahmung und des Begehrens: Materialien zu Gabriel Tarde. Frankfurt a.M., Suhrkamp, p. 10

14. Tarde, pp. 96 – 101

15. cf. Czarniawska, Barbara (2017). Organizational Change – Fashions. Institutions, and Translations. In: The Palgrave Handbook of Organizational Change Thinkers. Cham Palgrave Macmillan, pp. 361 – 377

16. cf. Lüdemann, Susanne (2009). Die imaginäre Gesellschaft. Gabriel Tardes antinaturalistische Soziologie der Nachahmung. In: Christian Borch & Urs Stäheli (Hrsg.). Soziologie der Nachahmung und des Begehrens – Materialien zu Gabriel Tarde. Frankfurt a.M., Suhrkamp

17. Lemke, Thomas (2013). Gesellschaftskörper und Organismuskonzepte: Überlegungen zur Bedeutung von Metaphern in der soziologischen Theo-rie. In: Die Natur in der Soziologie. Gesellschaftliche Voraussetzungen und Folgen biotechnologischen Wissens. Frankfurt a.M, Campus-Verl., pp. 84 – 106

18. cf. Lüdemann

19. cf. Czarniawska

20. Luhmann, Niklas (1997). Die Gesellschaft der Gesellschaft. Frankfurt a.M., Suhrkamp, p. 70 & 603

21. Borch, Christian (2009). Schaum-Organisationen: Über das Management von Atmosphären. In: Die Vermessung des Ungeheuren. Die Philosophie nach Peter Sloterdijk. Wilhelm Funk Verlag. pp. 375 – 376

22. Sloterdijk, Peter (2004). Sphären III – Schäume. Frankfurt a.M., Suhrkamp

23. ibid, p. 255 & 302

24. Funcke, Bettina (2005). Against Gravity. Bettina Funcke in conversation with Peter Sloterdijk. Link (07.20.2020) http://dev.autonomedia.org/node/4584

25. Tarde, p. 111

26. cf. Rogers, Everet M. (1995). Diffusion of innovation. New York, The Free Press

27. cf. Kinnunen, Jussi (1996). Gabriel Tarde as a founding father of innovation diffusion research. Acta Sociologica, Vol. 39, pp. 431 – 442

28. cf. Marsden, Paul (2000). Forefathers of Memetics: Gabriel Tarde and the Laws of Imitation. Journal of Mimetics-Evolutionary Models of Information Transmission, Vol. 4, n°1

29. Tarde, Gabriel de (1993). Les lois de l'imitation. Paris, Editions Kimé, p. 7

30. cf. Czarniawska, Barbara (2009). Gabriel Tarde and Organization Theory. In: Paul Adler (ed.). The Oxford Handbook of Sociology and Organization Studies: Classical Foundations. Oxford, Oxford University Press

31. Borch, Christian & Stäheli, Urs, pp. 10 – 11

32. ibid, p. 17

33. ibid, p. 16

34. Tarde, p. 31
35. cf. Saussure, Ferdinand de (1997). Linguistik und Semiologie. Notizen aus dem Nachlaß. Texte, Briefe und Dokumente, gesammelt, übersetzt und eingeleitet v. Johannes Fehr, Frankfurt/M., Suhrkamp, p. 255
36. Tarde, p. 31
37. Weik, Karl E. (1995). Sensemaking in Organizations. New York, Sage, p. 119
38. ibid, p. 15
39. Tarde, p. 36
40. cf. Tarde, Gabriel de (2009). Monadologie und Soziologie. Frankfurt a.M., Suhrkamp
41. cf. Hegele-Raih, Cornelia (2006). Was ist … Isomorphismus? In: Harvard Business Manager, link (07.20.2020): https://www.manager-magazin.de/harvard/print/hm/d-47632104.html
42. cf. Hargadon, Andrew B. & Yellowlees, Douglas (2001). When Innovations Meet Institutions: Edison and the Design of the Electric Light. In: Administrative Science Quarterly, September 2001, pp. 476 – 501
43. cf. Hegele-Raih
44. ibid
45. ibid
46. cf. Revell, Timothy (2018). How to stop artificial intelligence being so racist and sexist. In: newscientist.com, link (07.20.2020) https://www.newscientist.com/article/2173472-how-to-stop-artificial-intelligence-being-so-racist-and-sexist/#ixzz6SrqEGVjr
47. cf. Harari, Yuval Noah (2014). Sapiens: A Brief History of Humankind. London, Harvill Secker

From quotation to gesture

A completely new quality of codification, of the irrevocable and unmistakable, based on technology is represented by the blockchain. The authority over a consensus or an agreement resulting from it is thereby exercised decentrally.

The blockchain is a decentralised database whose data is managed and protected in a particularly secure way because it is distributed across different servers. Deviations and manipulations can therefore not be ruled out, but they are extremely unlikely because the information would have to be changed on all the computers involved, and not just on one. The blockchain is transparent and traceable for all users in a controlled way. If a contract is concluded there or a bank transfer is made, practically everyone knows this. Information stored in a blockchain cannot be changed or deleted by any central body. So, it's as if that information has been carved in stone. And from an economic perspective, the blockchain builds on an old economic principle: a public statement.

Strictly speaking, the blockchain also corresponds to Sloterdijk's foam concept with its co-fragility, since in this fabric every change can be perceived by everyone in some way and therefore no central supervision is necessary. However, there is a serious difference between the spatial metaphors of foamspace and blockchain: while foamspace permits discourse and the permanent social negotiation of circumstances, blockchain concentrates on the aspect of control. However, the fact that this control is exercised transparently and decentrally and that hierarchies as well as privileged mediators that exercise power can be overridden means that the blockchain is widely understood as a liberal achievement.

The blockchain combines aspects of the network that serve as an infrastructure to outline long-distance relationships and unexpected connections between local points and those of the spheres of Sloterdijk to describe local, fragile and complex "atmospheric conditions„. Bruno Latour notes in this context that the word "network" has become a ubiquitous term for technical infrastructures, social relations, geopolitics, the mafia and, of course, our new life online (1).

The first and still most popular application of the blockchain is the mining of crypto currencies. The organisation of work no longer focuses on cultivating fields, keeping animals or producing goods from raw materials with the help of machines, for example. Instead, it is directly focused on a technology that immediately produces monetary value with the help of an infrastructure and the use of energy.

Blockchain technologies such as crypto currencies can help shape our social world. These distributed applications have the potential to transform the very nature of organisation, our financial system, our bureaucracies and our governance models. Advancing the ontological question, we can postulate that the blockchain consists of programming code as a sequence of symbols that can be read by computing devices. However, this code has a significant human and indeed social–institutional dimension.

„All the world's a stage, and all the men and women merely players. " These words by Shakespeare remind us again of the importance of narratives that shape our lives and make us human (2). Although technologies have no consciousness, do not experience childlike imprinting, do not identify with archetypes, etc. and therefore do not produce stories themselves, humans have always packed them into our stories. Moreover, stories such as those of Daedalus or the moon landing by Jules Verne have spurred our imagination and made them into something like self-fulfilling prophecies. There are already technologies at work in our minds that may not even exist yet.

However, such ideas or visions do not arise by themselves and, as we have already seen, they also have references to the past. As Agre argues, technological developments are usually embedded in narrative structures that are not only technical, but also include collective ideas for forming our societies and institutional reality (3). If one understands the blockchain as a data structure intended to be unchangeable insofar as it is a cultural technique conceived by human beings in a long tradition of media technologies, our perception of it also changes: from the hand wedge to writing to book printing; these have served to open up the world. Nobody will deny that every medium also has an influence on development. At the same time, our greater cultural–historical zoom allows technology to be classified better (4).

From this cultural–historical perspective, it can be said that the blockchain combines the benefits of making something public over long distances – due to its electronic infrastructure – with the advantages of a material culture of writing, such as book printing, thereby creating a certain commitment between all stakeholders. However, for the majority of users who cannot code themselves, the code acting in the background is a kind of black box (5). Here we are again far behind the level of medieval monks, who belonged to a small elite of people who mastered the cultural technique of writing and reading.

This circumstance is also important because the blockchain is also equipped with rules for consensus. Public blockchains are structured as decentralised systems, and since they do not depend on a central governing body, the decentralised nodes must therefore agree on the validity of transactions. This is where consensus algorithms come into play. They ensure compliance with protocol rules and guarantee that all transactions are processed reliably, so that in the case of crypto currencies, for example, the coins can only be issued once (6).

It can be seen as problematic that the technological language of coding has so far only been mastered by a small group. Because codes also shape our view of the world. It is important to understand that codes not only represent "reality", but also give this construct a structure, one that manifests itself again in our narratives, even those of ourselves. Blockchain technologies are not just "narrative" in the sense that they are part of the stories we – as individuals, communities and societies – tell about them. Blockchain technologies can do much more: they can configure the narratives we use to interpret our everyday social reality (7)

However, it will probably be a long time before the cultural technique of coding can prepare data in such a way that we fully understand it and thus the world can be opened up even better for us humans as a collective. We don't have that much time because, depending on your perspective, we are giving up more and more of our interpretive sovereignty or creative power, when algorithms themselves write new algorithms.

In an optimistic scenario, based on historical experience, one might think that a development like that of writing is emerging. This was already in practice even before it could be used broadly. And when the majority could finally write, they made use of their right to personal exploration of the world and it wrote history itself.

With regard to this assessment, however, it must be said that, for example, the effects of printing have always found their way through our minds before actions have been taken that have changed reality. Today, the conceived codes are directly linked to the technologies of execution. It is therefore not guaranteed that a code as an interface between an algorithm and the computer that performs the calculation steps has been socially negotiated.

Based on Marshall McLuhan idea that technologies and also cultural techniques have a structural impact, this applies to writing and books as well as to coding and blockchains, and artificial intelligence, etc. Thus, with the printing of books, a structural power was probably exerted on society which the participants were also unaware of, since it was focused on the content of the communication in question.

Writing is an expression of our thinking, and it requires a reader who might be motivated to act as a reaction. And we should also not forget that there is more than one reader and therefore divergent interpretations of a text can also lead to different actions. Encoding is also an act similar to writing due to our thinking, but the programming code has to be seen as a speech act that is capable of directly constituting reality. In addition, previously established cultural techniques like writing, which have enabled us to negotiate our social reality, are increasingly coupled with such speech acts. This fact should not blind us to the classification of programming languages as formal languages, which are considered to be more precise and clearer in comparison to natural languages.

As a result, social relationships become more and more rigid, which leads to a loss of dynamism and thus to freedom and a sense of responsibility. Technologies like the blockchain configure narrative structures that are abstract from the realm of action. To do so, they construct quasi-entities in quasi-plots that represent events that actually happened (8).

„Then God said, 'Let there be light'; and there was light.„ Similarly, as described here in Genesis, the speech acts produced by the technique of coding work too. This scene from the Book of Creation represents a conception of writing in which letters are not merely linguistic symbols, but something real, consisting of a certain spiritual substance. For God, it is possible to arrange these letters according to his will so that, at the same time, something like reality arises from them (9).

These divine speech acts of creation history are something completely original. They come from nowhere and have no context to which they have been tied. They are a kind of happening, a pure event or *performance* (German: *Vorstellung*). If, as proclaimed in the Gospel of John, the Word marks the beginning of creation, then God also expresses Himself in it and manifests Himself in this creation. The execution of the spoken word as creation could be interpreted as a performative speech act in the sense of John Longshaw Austin (10). But it is inconceivable – at least for us humans – that God could already have an idea of what, according to this narrative, did not yet exist and what he was the first to initiate. This radical form of emergence exceeds our idea of imagination.

Our inability *to imagine* (German: sich vorstellen) that one is able to imagine what has not yet existed may also be expressed in the following: If we remember Tarde and the laws of *imitation* (German: Nachahmung), it

89

is remarkable that the concept of imitation is derived from *creation* (German: Schöpfung) with regard to its origin. The term "ahmen" or "amen" derives from the Middle High German term for a hollow measure or a liquid measure for wine that had to be *drawn* (German: geschöpft) from a barrel. *Drawing* (German: Schöpfung), which we associate with creativity in its alternative meaning, is thus associated with a measure. In every act of creation, we see rules and standards in the background. This could be similar in other languages in relation to the word "imitation", whose origin can be traced back to "aim", which also means the production of an artificial similarity, a copy, and formerly also served as a term for "calculating".

A core question that is derived from this is which forms of radical action and performative agitation remain possible in our digitalised and mediatised organisations? What scope for action is still available in our working world as a horizon in the digital smog of e-mail correspondence, the intranet and the newsletters that come crashing down on us? Beyond the permanent quoting and repetition of norms and conventions, which thereby gain authority and lead to their consolidation in society, is there also the possibility of modifying discourses?

Norms and conventions become more solid in the course of time and acquire certain meanings. Judith Butler speaks here of sedimentation or materialisation (11). Butler's work on the historical nature of norms and conventions, which are apparent in gender identity, for example, derives from Jacques Derrida's analysis of the functionality of signs. According to Derrida, signs are understandable only because they are repeatable (12). Judith Butler constantly emphasises the non-existence of the original as such. The ideal is attempted to be achieved performatively, but only an approximation is possible (13).

Social norms and conventions shape us before we even notice it. Yet according to Butler, our actions are not predetermined. Precisely because the convention as such must be confirmed again and again, there are also ways of refusing, ignoring or undermining these confirmations. In this, Butler sees, despite the analysis, that norms are violent ascriptions, which in principle show the ability to act. But what happens when the norms become weaker? If the authorities that safeguard practice no longer appear to be valid; what happens to action then?

These questions are also important because, for Butler, identity is not exclusively the direct cause of actions, behaviour and gestures, but conversely, these performative acts can also have an identity-defining character. They define our identity and maintain this social construct by constantly reconfiguring it from these actions.

This is where the identity-giving and insofar productive character of the performative meets the productive moment of power, as seen in the work of Michel Foucault. Here, too, we are dealing with a reversal of circumstances: It is not knowledge that produces power, but power that produces a certain knowledge. For Foucault, power is no longer interested in the destruction and annihilation of individuals, but in the production of reality and the constitution of the individual with his/her corporeality and his/her knowledge (14). At this point, therefore, it is no longer a question of the mere ability of an individual, but also of the will and the assertiveness of ability in a group, in a community and in an organisation.

References:
1. Latour, Bruno (2015). Some experiments in art and politics. In: Aranda J, Wood BK, Vidokle A (eds.) The Internet does not exist – e-flux Journal, Berlin, Sternberg Press, pp. 40 – 53
2. Shakespeare, William (1623). As you like it. London, Penguin Books, p. 52
3. Agre, P.E.(2003). Peer-to-Peer and the Promise of Internet Equality.Communications of the ACM,46(2), p. 39 – 42
4. cf. Reijers, Wessel & Coeckelbergh, Mark (2018). The Blockchain as a Narrative Technology: Investigating the Social Ontology and Normative Configurations of Cryptocurrencies. Philos. Technol. 31, pp. 103 – 130
5. ibid, pp. 122 – 125
6. ibid, pp. 103 – 107
7. ibid, pp. 106 – 110
8. ibid, pp. 109 – 121
9. Blumenthal, David R. 1980: Understanding Jewish Mysticism. In History, Religion, and Spiritual Democracy: Essays in Honor of Joseph L. Blau. Ed. M. Wohlgelernter, New York, Columbia University Press, pp. 114 – 115
10. cf. Austin, John Longshaw (1972). Zur Theorie der Sprechakte (How to do things with Words). Deutsche Bearbeitung von Eike von Savigny. Stuttgart, Reclam
11. cf. Butler, Judith (1993). Bodies that Matter: On the discursive limits of "sex". New York, London: Routledge, p. 15
12. cf. Derrida, Jacques (2001). "Signatur Ereignis Kontext". In: Limited Inc. Hrsg. von Peter Engelmann. Wien, Passagen, pp. 27 – 28
13. Gebske, Jennifer (2009). Performativität zwischen Zitation und Ereignis. Vergleich der Performativitätsbegriffe von Judith Butler und Erika Fischer-Lichte. Magisterarbeit, Friedrich-Alexander-Universität Erlangen-Nürnberg, p. 18
14. Duschlbauer, Thomas (2001). Medien und Kultur im Zeitalter der X-Kommunikation. Wien, Braumüller, p. 33

From capability to will

So far, we have stayed with organisations in terms of the skills and knowledge of their members and have looked at the role they will play in a thoroughly digitalised world. We have also looked at the scope for action by the employees, which can serve to test them and further develop their skills.

Recently, we have seen that this constant testing can not only lead to products and services changing and innovating in small steps, but also to the people within an organisation acquiring a new self-conception. The latter sounds tempting for the organisation, in so far as it could try to instrumentalise and embrace this process entirely for itself and the goal of profit maximisation. So perhaps all that is needed is some kind of coaching to make the employees feel themselves again and to discover their existing potential and make it usable for the organisation. In addition, perhaps a weekly fruit basket and free entry to a fitness studio would be of benefit.

But wait a minute: What if these freedoms turn out to be a Pandora's box, especially since we don't know what ideas the employees might come up with and if they will actually help the organisation's objectives? What if these freedoms even end up with employees not only changing the taste of a chocolate bar or the design of a toothbrush, for example, but also questioning the "design" of their organisation with its business model, processes, departments, etc.? What if this enthusiasm manifests itself in a way that is no longer beneficial to the body of an organisation? What if not only the beautiful messages of marketing are spread virally, but also this form of negotiating meaning within an organisation spreads like a virus, infecting more and more employees? What if parts of the organisation see that their activity is actually useless, that their skills might be much better off in another organisation or that this "host animal" called organisation is not even needed for them to survive as individuals?

Therefore, the organisation sees itself well advised to be open to new things, but at the same time to establish an immune system against all those who might radically question it. Therefore, it is not surprising that those very companies that always carry the blessings of disruptive innovation like a monstrance have learned over time what it means to act and react in a way that stabilises the system. Agile leadership or New Work are only two terms in this context which may mean something completely different than they claim to, quite simply because there is, and perhaps even must be, an understanding of what freedom can ultimately do to an organisation.

Freedom of thought and action, which can manifest itself, for example, through unbridled creativity or breaches of rules, can lead to undreamt-of competitive advantages on the one hand, but on the other hand can lead directly to disaster. The former is praised again and again; the latter is latently inscribed in the memory of an organisation and remains unmentioned to the outside world. The former serves as our motivation and is publicly in the spotlight; the latter is often associated with so-called failure and is addressed reluctantly.

So, it is no wonder that organisations in the sense of the body metaphor here obviously assume something pathological. A little bit of illness and infection is quite permissible, even desirable, because it increases immunity and strengthens the organisation in the concept of the survival of the fittest. However, a certain amount of control and precautions for containment are always required. It is necessary to be able to identify potential pathogens (German: "Erreger" – exciters) in order to either remove them, marginalise them or put them in a kind of quarantine.

This is why the organisation is not only focused on freedom, the Agon or fair competition for the better argument among equals and the question of the special abilities of the employees, but also on control, power and willpower. An organisation is therefore not always a petting zoo, but often a shark tank. Not everything is subject to rationally comprehensible considerations, but there are also forces and dynamics that operate with moods, emotions and affects in order to impose a point of view and exercise power.

This, too, cannot be thought of as completely detached from the style phenomenon, since it is the art critic Susan Sontag who refers to the will in this context. In her reflections on style, she places the will at the centre of our perception and our epistemological decisions, because she speaks of the fact that a work of art allows us to see and understand something unique, but not to evaluate and generalise. This act of understanding, accompanied by a desire, is for her the only purpose and convincing justification of a work of art (1).

Sontag sees the best way to shed light on the nature of our experience of art and the relationship between art and the rest of human feeling and doing is to bring the concept of the will to our aid. This term is useful because the will is not only a specific attitude of consciousness, a tensioned consciousness, as it were. It also characterises an attitude towards the world, an attitude of a subject towards the world. Inspired by Nietzsche's "The Birth of Tragedy", art is not about imitating nature and reality, but about overcoming them and creating a complement as an individual creation (2).

Accordingly, art is the objectification of the will in a thing or performance and the provocation or awakening of the will. From the point of view of the artist, it is the creation of an imaginary decoration for the will. Sontag links the stylistic complexity that has emerged from this with the unprecedented technical development of human will using technology and the tremendous commitment of the will towards a new form of social and psychological order, an order based on infinite change (3). We see, therefore, that the will to overcome nature and reality, rather than the desire to imitate them, is in its infancy. Only then do the imitations emerge, when it is operationally a question of the use of technologies, about improvements and change.

Hence, although stylistic decisions can always be traced back to any historical developments – such as the invention of writing, the printing press or digitalisation – and this is certainly well-founded; when viewed purely superficially or from a historical perspective, this always remains undifferentiated and is only aimed at epochs, traditions and schools. If, on the other hand, one looks at art from within and tries to determine the reasons for its value and effect in an individual work of art, one discovers an element of coincidence in every stylistic decision – however justified it may seem. If art is a sublime game that the will plays with itself, then "style" consists of a set of rules according to which this game plays itself out. And the rules are ultimately always an artificial and accidental limitation, whether they are rules of form or rules that determine the existence of certain contents (4).

For Sontag, style is usually only revealed to the viewer through the repetition of a work or the act of recognising those similarities that remain dominant in an artist's creative process despite ongoing changes (5). Style is therefore also a method of highlighting for easier assignment. It will therefore be noticed that stylistic choices, by concentrating our attention on some things, limit this attention at the same time, forbid us to perceive others. In the strictest sense, all contents of consciousness are unnameable. Even the simplest perception is indescribable in its totality. Every work of art must therefore be understood not only as something represented, but also simultaneously as an attempt – to use Wittgenstein's words – to express the unspeakable. In the great works of art, therefore, there is always something vibrating that cannot be put into words and that can also be described as the sublime. Stylistic means are also always methods of avoidance, which is why the most effective element is often silence.

What is also remarkable about Susan Sontag's analysis of style is that although she refers to art, she explicitly notes that style is a term that can be applied to any way we experience it – as often as we speak of its forms and qualities. Many works of art, which very well deserve our interest, must be considered inconsistent by this standard, whereas many objects of our experience, which are not classified as works of art, have some of the qualities of an object of art. Whenever language, movement, behaviour or objects show a certain deviation from the most direct, useful and uncommitted way of expression and being in the world, we can say of them that they have „style„, that they are autonomous and exemplary (6)

If we follow these remarks on style, taking into account the importance of the will, a further differentiation arises here between the dogma, which is regarded as imperative, and the style: we have already noted that the style does not exist as the opposite of the dogma and have also suspected a connection between the two. The dogma exists as a clear regulation, but its observance can be interpreted more or less arbitrarily, as we know, for example, from the time of the Inquisition. The style, on the other hand, seems to us to be arbitrary from the outset, although there is a set of rules behind it. But we only become aware of this through repetitions and variations. Ultimately, however, it is probably just as difficult or even impossible to follow a dogma with clear rules accurately as it is to imitate a style whose rules are hidden to us.

Susan Sontag, however, refers not only to the meaning of desire and will, but also to the methods and techniques by which we try to form style as an overcoming of reality, and through which a wealth of expressions is created. The use of techniques is not just limited to the creation of art, but is also related to us, especially if we assume that performative actions constantly shape our self or identity. When we turn to Michel Foucault, for example, then we can find the notion of technologies of the self, conscious and intentional practices, whereby people not only define the rules of their behaviour, but also try to modify themselves and create a work from their lives that embodies particular aesthetic values and meets certain stylistic criteria (7). These are thus concrete strategies for action and ways for shaping life, with which the subject can constitute itself. The individual applies practices to him/herself in order to achieve a certain goal, each of which is connected to his/her historically and socially specific location, i.e. is a consequence of the power that can be felt in everyday life.

What is now exciting in connection with the technologies of the self is the question of to what extent these individual processes now happen voluntarily or through compulsion, or to what extent we actually act autonomously in "our" decisions. This question is exciting for several reasons: In terms of organisations, we should not only know where we can locate abilities, but also where and how the power is exercised that helps people to make use of their skills or to let them wither away. We need to know much more about the real will and desire of people, because in the sense of New Work New Culture, for example, there is a need for organisations that encourage their employees to do what they "really, really" want (8).

In general, Foucault sketches two central components of the development of power: On the one hand, disciplinary power starts with the individual body, in order to direct itself as a regulatory power in the form of "biopolitics" towards the social body as a whole. Both components are not only logically interrelated, but also in a thoroughly practical relationship. The respective power technologies build on each other: The disciplining of the individual body is to a certain extent the prerequisite for the enforcement of those biopolitical measures of controlling the population as 'mass effects'. On this basis, the question of 'governmentality' gains in importance, i.e. the question of how techniques of domination make use of the processes in which individuals influence themselves and, vice versa, how these technologies of the self are integrated into power and domination structures. The technologies of the self are also always an element of the technologies of government, of domination, in that they influence the relationship between the individual's self-management and management by others. The social implementation and enforcement of technologies of the self – in the sense of self-management, of autonomy and self-control – is thus an integral part of the domination dispositive of modern societies, whose functional conditions are linked to the existence of certain forms of subjectivity (9).

This idea of the dispositive (10) allows us to question more systematically theoretically and more precisely empirically that previously asserted entanglement of – or the grey area between – totalisation and autonomisation. Dispositives are regarded as 'infrastructures' of dominant orders of knowledge, which in turn, on the basis of discursive truth politics, determine with their validated knowledge what we should perceive or consider to be true – and thus orient and standardise our actions. The emergence of dispositives is contingent, but not accidental, because they are problem-related – that is, they bundle all those discursive truths, activities, regulatory services and the corresponding institutional practices, such as material artifacts, that are directed at coping with a social 'emergency', an 'urgance'. With this dispositive concept, discourses, practices, institutions, etc. can thus be regarded as components of "power strategies" (11).

If we want to know more precisely how exactly this modulation between self-development and standardisation and between fun and performance works within organisations, then together with Foucault we should again turn to the metaphors of illness and infection. This may seem to be a bit far away from the reality of an organisation, and Foucault's „excursions„ into the history of mental homes, clinics and the penal system may even seem disturbing to us when it comes to understanding the nature of an organisation. However, recent events around Covid-19, for example, have shown what forms of power and control are possible and practised today; and how people react to them. We also find it difficult to differentiate between what was „prescribed„ by an authority and what was „voluntarily„ undertaken to contain the pandemic, especially since even people who had no official mandate for control spontaneously took on surveillance or police functions.

In "Discipline and Punish", Foucault distinguishes between two models of the exercise of power with regard to the containment of infectious diseases, which emerged from this and converged in the 19th century (12). As we shall see, they are more relevant than ever before, even for the description of today's organisations. On the one hand, there were the exclusion rituals with which leprosy was reacted to. To a certain extent, they gave up the model of confinement in the 17th century and symbolise the visions of a pure society, in which the sick or deviating individual is excluded, banned and marginalised.

On the other hand, the plague has given rise to a model of disciplining which, instead of the massive and dichotomous drawing of boundaries, calls for individualised divisions, for an all-encompassing and deep organisation of surveillance. The person suffering from the plague is not banished together with his fellow sufferers; instead, he is individually differentiated and carefully seized by a power that divides and multiplies (13). In the case of leprosy, marginalisation and separation is de facto a form of outsourcing from the body of the city, while the plague made it necessary to have subtle segmentation, to divide the city into different quarantine zones and to differentiate more strongly. *"The exile of the leper and the arrest of the plague do not bring with them the same political dream. The first is that of a pure community, the second that of a disciplined society. Two ways of exercis-*

ing power over men, of controlling their relations, of separating out their dangerous mixtures." (14)

In recent years, we have been able to witness these two processes very impressively with the refugee crisis and the Covid-19 virus. On the one hand, people at the borders or in the Mediterranean Sea were treated like lepers, and on the other hand we could observe the segmentation and isolation of people in quarantine.

The extent to which the two models have come closer together – or more precisely, how much they complement each other – is also evident from the monitoring bodies: *"Treat 'lepers' as 'plague victims', project the subtle segmentations of discipline onto the confused space of internment, combine it with the methods of analytical distribution proper to power, individualize the excluded, but use procedures of individualisation to mark exclusion – this is what was operated regularly by disciplinary power from the 'beginning of the nineteenth century in the psychiatric asylum, the penitentiary, the reformatory, the approved school and, to some extent, the hospital."* (15)

For Foucault, the paradigm of disciplinary technologies that emerged from this approach is represented by the Bentham model of the Panopticon, in which a real or even imaginary guard in it can monitor the occupants of the cells arranged in a circle around it from an elevated position – without being seen. This architectural model, designed by Jeremy Bentham in 1787, was intended not only for prisons, but also for hospitals, factories and schools. For if it protects delinquents from bad mutual influences and from new criminal plans, then there is no danger of infection among the sick, there is no brawling, theft and distractions among workers that disturb and delay work, and there is no noise, gossip and copying among students. The manifold exchange within a densely packed mass, the fusion of individuality, all these collective effects are replaced in the Panopticon by a collection of separate, atomised individuals. From the perspective of the warden, it is a matter of a controlled and countable diversity; from that of the inmates, of an observed and imposed loneliness (16).

In the Panopticon, the original principle of the dungeon with its three functions of confinement, concealment and obscuration is partially reversed by the glaring backlighting and the gaze of the observer. The main effect is the creation of a permanent and conscious state of visibility in the prisoner, which guarantees the automatic functioning of power. Even if the execution is only sporadic, the surveillance still has a permanent effect. The perfection thus achieved allows the power to make its actual exercise superfluous. It is latently present, constantly visible, but completely invisible. The delinquent always has to reckon with being monitored at any moment (17). The subject will therefore behave correspondingly differently in the Panopticon than in a dark dungeon, as we still know from Ludwig van Beethoven's Fidelio, for example.

This disciplinary technology has gained importance mainly because it de-individualises and automates power. Moreover, the one who is exposed to visibility and knows this, takes over the means of coercion and plays them off against himself; he internalises the power relationship in which he plays both roles. Thanks to its subtle observation mechanisms, the Panopticon, which functions as a kind of laboratory of power, thus gains in effectiveness and diffuses ever more deeply into the behaviour of those affected. In every application, this surveillance apparatus allows the perfection of the exercise of power because it allows increasingly fewer people to exercise power over ever more people (18).

In addition, because of its anonymous character, anyone can exercise power within the Panopticon. De-individualisation, automation and anonymity thus contribute significantly to the fact that this model can be integrated into any function (19). Education, healing, punishment and production are just a few examples of what can be done with this instrument. Moreover, the Panopticon can enhance any function by intimately merging with it; it can constitute a mixed system in which power and knowledge relationships are precisely and intimately aligned with the processes to be controlled. It can establish a direct relationship between power and an increase in production (20).

Foucault doesn't stop here though. He tries to convince us that Bentham's Panopticon, no matter how inadequately realised, is only the miniature edition that reflects the widespread trend towards surveillance in bourgeois society. Overall, the Panopticon was only a vivid example of "panoptism", the modern bourgeois culture's political dream of a disciplined society (21). By depriving diversity of a quantity useful to society, a composite force that is greater than a simple sum, the Panopticon contributes to growth (22).

It is therefore not surprising that disciplinary mechanisms are beginning to expand beyond the institution of the Panopticon. For economic motives, such as helping and encouraging people to work, but also for religious motives, such as conversion, the fight against immorality and fornication, as well as for political considerations, such as the avoidance of riots, initiatives are founded which, under the pretext of "caring", ultimately aim to discipline society – especially its underprivileged classes.

The network of disciplinary procedures is not only becoming increasingly dense from the closed institutions, which are beginning to accumulate information about society, but also from these associations and initiatives (23). In the interest of health, reproduction, the future of the species and the vitality of the social body, power takes care of the body of individuals and becomes the normative control of life ("bio-power"). For Foucault, the maxim of state rationality or the modern art of government is therefore to develop the constitutive elements of the lives of individuals in such a way that this process also promotes those of governmental authority (24).

The prevailing disciplinary mechanisms lead to a fundamental change in the structure of society. More than the legal theorists and philosophers of the 18th century, it is likely that the military and technicians of discipline contributed to the constitution of the new model of society. For Foucault, the modern individual is a product of these disciplinary technologies, for which s/he is both an object and an instrument. The identification and classification mechanisms of justice, police, medicine and psychiatry are thus the birthplace of the predictable subject (25).

In Foucault's analysis, this subjugation of the body forms the substructure of representational democracy, although democratic freedoms tend to be suspended (26): And even if the universally valid legal system of modern society seems to place limits on the exercise of power, its omnipresent panoptism, in contrast to law, keeps in motion a machine that is both incalculable and inconspicuous, which supports, reinforces, multiplies and undermines the asymmetry of the powers that be. The inconspicuous disciplines, the everyday panoptisms may lie below the big apparatuses and below the big political struggles: In the genealogy of modern society, they, together with the class domination that crossed them, formed the counterpart of the legal norms of power distribution (27).

The Panopticon thus epitomises the universal, hidden, autonomous and effective "microphysics of power", which creates mute, docile and productive bodies that prove the success of drilling by becoming the subjects of the disciplining power technologies, e.g. In the process of testing (28), evaluations and rankings.

This kind of surveillance still functions according to similar principles today. And it continues to be about power. China's social scoring system is perhaps the best-known example of how far technology can be advanced to not only track but also influence individual behaviour. As we have seen, surveillance technology has long been accessible only to governments, but private companies are now increasingly using it in the workplace. Video surveillance, computers and other digital technologies are now routinely used in many places to monitor employee performance and control behaviour. With artificial intelligence and facial recognition, surveillance could soon be expanded to include behaviour and private matters such as health. When asked about this topic, employees describe digital surveillance as a major concern. A survey conducted in the UK by the trade union Prospect shows that more than half of the 7,500 members surveyed consider it likely that they will be routinely monitored at work (29). In the case of workers in home care and public employment services, the European Public Service Union describes in a report that the second biggest impact of digitisation in these areas is the increased surveillance of work and workers. Similar concerns are shared by the European Transport Association (30).

Surveillance can take extreme forms, for example by using algorithms and AI systems without workers being aware of it. In the case of so-called "people analytics", for example, such software allows companies to fully monitor and analyse what their employees are doing at their desks. For example, a company like ActivTrack offers employee monitoring and behavioural analysis using machine learning. CleverControl is a cloud-based solution that promises total control over employees' computers and the ability to track down lazybones. Spyrix Software advertises its wealth of functions: keylogging, screen capturing, webcam and microphone recording, monitoring of websites and social applications. Time Doctor even promises behaviour correction: This is because the software helps to ensure that employees work the full number of hours and do not interrupt them by wasting their working time for the company, for example with Facebook activities.

Monitoring entails immediate risks such as discrimination, invasion of privacy and data protection by failing to obtain informed consent. There is also the threat of a Big Brother-like look over the shoulders of employees and a violation of their rights to information, consultation and participation. Other risks include the loss of autonomy and personal freedom and an increase in stress levels, which would bring us back to the Panopticon. While we or our behaviour is fully visible, much remains hidden to us. Although everything seems to be accessible to us at any time on the Internet, we have no insight into the algorithms that determine the order of the information or that can simply withhold certain information. Here we stand in front of a black box. Especially in view of the abundance of information, we cannot even begin to guess what information would actually be important for us. That is why many people retreat to the belief that a really relevant message will find its way to them anyway (31).

Such excesses of digital surveillance and inequality in terms of transparency may also affect an operational organisation, as can be seen from these examples. However, this contradicts the friendly face that an organisation would like to maintain in order to be attractive as an employer brand and to retain employees. In this respect, there is a need for another element that works on a more subtle and therefore far more productive level.

For Foucault, power shows itself less from its destructive side, but rather from a productive one. In general, destruction exists in our post-capitalist society almost exclusively in connection with forms of recycling. The total annihilation means the loss of control, because the annihilated cannot be tracked down anywhere or made useful because of its nullity. Power does not destroy but transforms, and therefore managers do not speak of crises but only sense opportunities for change (32).

To get to the core of this development, the connection between power and knowledge must be emphasised, because knowledge is based on information. The new information technologies enable a so-called explosion of knowledge, which defines the current subject (33). The relationship between knowledge and power is often reduced and trivialised in a slogan-like form to Francis Bacon's "Knowledge is power". In his analysis of power, Foucault therefore places a hyphen between the two terms, and with the term "power-knowledge" he wants to oppose the tradition of epistomology, which is guided by the idea that knowledge generally arises where power relations are suspended, that knowledge can only develop outside of power interests. Rather, the self is a tool of power to produce knowledge that is arbitrary or useful to it. With the discovery or rather a construction of the self at the beginning of the Enlightenment, its taking possession has obviously also begun. Physical repression, the wounding, dissection and destruction of the human body, was finally replaced by its (human-)scientifically based utilisation for the purpose of power over access to the self (34). Foucault postulates that power is not conceived in the alternative: violence or ideology. In fact, every point of the exercise of power is a place of knowledge formation at the same time. And conversely, all established knowledge allows and ensures the exercise of power (35).

The individual is already a fabrication, a synthetic reality produced by a specific "power-knowledge". This technology of power, consisting of classification, surveillance, disciplining, normalisation, etc. does not leave the objects to which it refers untouched. Its productive character consists mainly in the fact that power technology creates an environment in which something flourishes in its light (36). Thus, power must make enormous efforts to achieve positive effects at the level of desire. It takes an incredible amount of time and energy, it takes a lot of organisation to bring us up to the norm, to awaken a desire in us that can never be satisfied. In the narrower sense, the norm is a salvation, which is generated by procedural normative rationality. It does not obey any principle or myth and is a procedural regulation that began its triumphal march with the Enlightenment technology (37.

This manifestation of our normativity is criticised not only by Foucault, but also by representatives of other traditions, including Max Weber (38). Foucault's concept of power is particularly easy to grasp in the image of a network of relationships in which all take their place as supervised monitors; power cannot be localised in the function of a government, a leader, etc. Inevitably the norm establishes itself as a new type of power. Individuals are continually rewarded, corrected or punished in the course of their existence; any deviation from the rule, from "normal" behaviour is soon recognised by them as an error and is thus internalised. Thus, the norm is to be seen both as an instrument and as a product of the exercise of power (39).

The new information technologies afford us the power to extend the hegemony of the norm to all areas of life and to align the intentions and motivations of people. Advertising, public relations and statistical forecasts create the ideals that everyone has to follow. However, responsibility always falls back on the individual, who feels free but in principle acts in conformity (40).

Since power is to be regarded as a factor of production in this perspective, repression is considered more a subordinate means of implementing what is feasible. Incentive, seduction, compulsion and prohibition are expressed above all in the suggestive qualities of power: For if power were only to perform suppressive functions, if it were only to work in the manner of censorship, exclusion, shutting off, repression, in the manner of a great super-ego, if it were only to be exercised in a negative way, it would be fragile (41).

Foucault therefore also turns the dictum of the war theorist Clausewitz around and says that the peace currently practised is only a pseudo-form of peace and merely the continuation of war by other means. This war is a silent and secret civil war. It manifests itself in the conflicts over social institutions, economic inequalities, in our language and even in ourselves (42). In view of such a scenario, which actually assumes a permanent state of war, the distinction between "good" and "bad" information, between enlightenment and manipulation or propaganda, between objectivity and subjectivity can naturally no longer be maintained. If the implosion of opposites occurs here, then the information should also no longer be seen as a mere transfer of meaning or sense from A to B, but as a form of relationship. Information is not simply transferred like a cold. It is, as Marshall McLuhan put it, not only content but also form. Information can thus be described as a complex principle of order.

In relation to power, information therefore takes on the status of a supplement. Through this close entanglement, it simultaneously serves as its addition and its substitute. Identity and difference therefore characterise the interrelation between the two terms. Information has a central meaning for power because it can decentralise itself through it (43).

As regards such conditions, Gilles Deleuze presents a picture of the system of corruption of the human body, whereby it is obvious that there is a total and global vision on the side of power. This means that from the perspective of power, all the manifold repressions easily come together to form a whole (44). But what do such forms of "repression" look like in organisations today? How does the perspective of power and control shape itself here, when there is allegedly so much freedom and so little hierarchy in companies? What does this possibly have to do with the forms of agility and the much-heralded spirit of "New Work"?

Thus, in the world of organisations, we are not only experiencing the excesses of an almost total form of surveillance by the technologies of digitalisation, but we are also confronted here with exactly the two mechanisms that Foucault presents to us as the origin of the Panopticon. The difference here is that it is no longer a medieval urban body, as with the plague and leprosy, but we must once again metaphorically regard an organisation as an organ that must be protected from infections, pathogens and ulcers. These "diseases" are now embodied by the dangers of creativity and an unbridled spirit of innovation. Both must be controlled and safely instrumentalised in a world of volatility, uncertainty, complexity and ambiguity (VUCA), in other words a world of constant change. However, this control must be designed in such a way that it does not restrict motivation and productivity, and internalised by those involved in such a way that they exercise it against themselves as far as possible. Only in this way can the entrepreneurial risks for the organisation be reduced to a tolerable level.

The first mechanism, which is related to Foucault's findings, is to be found in an agile organisation, which is oriented towards self-control and self-organisation. All its processes and structures are designed to react as quickly as possible to unexpected challenges, events and opportunities. To this end, people with appropriate skills form teams that work together on the basis of agile values, principles and practices. Companies that are already feeling the volatility and dynamics of the markets today use these or similar forms of organisation. With a cell- and role-based organisation, a company focuses on self-responsibility and agility: Old hierarchical structures are abolished. The quintessential manager no longer exists. Every employee is equally responsible and now takes on self-chosen roles in which he or she has fun and is competent. Each cell has a purpose and goals to achieve and each business cell has its own profit and loss statement. A top circle synchronises and votes. The cell structure is also advantageous in terms of monitoring because the units can be clearly distinguished from one another. If a cell does not bring the expected benefit or even calls into question the success of the entity, it can be immediately isolated or eliminated. This model may be compared to that of segmentation in times of plague.

The other mechanism works within the model of the incubator: The aim of the company is to develop scalable business models together with the local start-ups and subsequently bring them onto the market. To achieve this, the company uses its internal and external network of experts. They work together on both the technical solutions and the strategic business model. However, the company not only contributes know-how and execution excellence, but also provides capital, for example in the form of a stake. Here the detachment is even greater than with the agile structures of an organisation. Creativity and inventiveness are outsourced in this model. As with leprosy colonies, the potential threateners are located outside a protective membrane. Due to this marginalisation of evil, the risk of failure remains to a large extent with the start-up's entrepreneurs.

Of course, in the context of globalisation, digitalisation, demographic change, the knowledge society and challenges such as climate change and a shortage of resources, it is comprehensible that organisations are testing and adopting new structures and that the work environment is changing radically as a result. While work at the beginning of the last century was increasingly associated with monotonous assembly line work, the professional life of employees today is also becoming increasingly complex, dynamic and confusing. Labour is undergoing major changes and work processes are becoming more transparent and highly adaptable. It is these developments that are changing our current image of work and also have an impact on the necessary qualifications of employees.

In order to meet these challenges, besides agile organisation, many methods, measures and opinions can be found under the keyword "New Work". However, at the core of the issue is that machines, together with algorithms, will probably be able to perform certain tasks better than humans in the future, which is why we should start to think even more intensively about the meaning of work. If work no longer needs us, what do we need work for? In this respect, New Work describes an epochal upheaval that begins with the question of meaning and transforms the world of work from the ground up. New Work focuses on the development of the potential of each individual person. Because work is at the service of mankind: We no longer work to live, and we no longer live to work. In the future, it will be all about the successful symbiosis of living and working. Rigid, hierarchical and authoritarian leadership concepts are therefore increasingly considered obsolete and will be replaced by modern, collaborative forms of cooperation.

The concepts of the New Work movement do not only confuse conventional organisations. Many of these interpretations of New Work, originally conceived as a social utopia by Frithjof Bergmann, also lose sight of the focus on people. After all, New Work has existed for more than 40 years: The Austro-American social philosopher Frithjof Bergmann has shaped this concept of New Work. He assumes that the previous work system is outdated because our society is in transition from an industrial to a knowledge society. As a result, traditional work structures are also changing and becoming more flexible. This affects both workspaces and working hours as well as corporate structures (45).

Before New Work mutated into a fashionable term – already partially devoid of meaning – and people began to seriously believe that table soccer and fruit baskets could solve the fundamental problems of corporate culture, it was originally called "New Work, New Culture" for a reason. The fundamental problem with today's interpretations of New Work, which apparently has to get by without a concept of culture, is probably also that most people who deal with it professionally in management consultancy do not know, understand or want to apply Bergmann's philosophical explanations around the concept of freedom. In these writings, Frithjof Bergmann refers to the thesis that people not only want freedoms, but also to exchange them for security. In his view, there is also a longing for miracles, mystery and the authority associated with them (46). This is also valid for an operational organisation. Otherwise, it would be highly surprising that, professionally, people regard themselves as free spirits, while, politically, they are currently increasingly joining authoritarian and populist movements. This is also because the concept of freedom is given enormous importance in our society, but one cannot feed on freedom. Freedom is a fundamental value of modern democracies, but it is not yet a guarantee that all problems can be solved automatically.

Given the transformation towards a knowledge economy, it is undisputed that labour will continue to change due to digitisation, as Bergmann predicted decades ago. Attitudes towards work have also changed – young people today have a different idea of work than their parents. Where hierarchies used to dominate, today it is all about networks. The closed back room is becoming an open space. Freedom, transparency, self-determination, but also responsibility demand great things from employees, managers and employers. Individuals are already advanced in their thinking, but organisations are not yet. According to Mark Poppenborg, the entrepreneur and founder of the think tank intrinsify, New Work is not a programme that can be introduced, but a bracket for a profound change in the economy (47).

Social networks are probably suitable as models for the new forms of cooperation. Following the model of Facebook, Twitter and Co., virtual business networks and social collaboration platforms such as Jive, Yammer, Sharepoint or Communote enable the networking of knowledge beyond company boundaries. This opens up scope for bringing together the right experts depending on the task at hand. At the same time, it also makes work mobile. In theory, it can take place almost anywhere and with anyone, but this also calls into question the traditional concept of an organisation.

On the other hand, especially where digitisation is taking hold in organisations, many things are no longer questioned in detail. For example, digitisation not only leads to an increase in bullshit jobs, it also opens up opportunities for those affected to get involved and, in the sense of radical constructivism, to create a world in which the full erosion potential of such jobs is not apparent.

While topics such as New Work or agile leadership are still associated with adhocracy or a form of organisation that is supposed to function without bureaucracy as far as possible, Chris Bilton already speaks of a "posthocracy" in connection with this radical constructivism, which is essentially based on trial and error and language games. In contrast to adhocracy with elements such as analysis, decisions and the attempt to position oneself, the focus here is on smaller steps, gestures and selecting from as many options as possible (48), but also the creation of alternative facts. For Bilton *"It favours decisive action and counters unpredictability with arbitrary certainties. In this respect, posthocracy mimics the visionary confidence of the heroic, differentiated strategy, a model based on charisma, individual insight and bold leaps of faith. The difference is that in a posthocracy analysis takes place after the decision, not before it."* (49)

107

References:
1. Sontag, Susan (1990). Against Interpretation, New York, Picador, p. 39
2. ibid, p. 39
3. ibid, p. 42
4. ibid, pp. 42 – 43
5. ibid, p. 45
6. cf. Sontag
7. Foucault, Michel (1986). Der Gebrauch der Lüste. Sexualität und Wahrheit 2. Band. Frankfurt a.M., Suhrkamp, p. 18
8. cf. Bergmann, Frithjof (2019). New Work New Culture, Work We Want And A Culture That Strengthens Us. Winchester, Washington, John Hunt Publishing, zero books
9. Hirseland, Andreas & Schneider, Werner (2008). Biopolitik und Technologien des Selbst: zur Subjektivierung von Macht und Herrschaft. In: K.-S. Rehberg (Hrsg.). Die Natur der Gesellschaft: Verhandlungen des 33. Kongresses der Deutschen Gesellschaft für Soziologie in Kassel 2006. Teilbd. 1 u. 2 (pp. 5640 – 5648). Frankfurt a. M., Campus Verl. P. 5643
10. cf. Foucault, Michel (1978). Dispositive der Macht. Über Sexualität, Wissen und Wahrheit. Berlin, Merve
11. Seier, Andrea (1999). Kategorien der Entzifferung: Macht und Diskurs als Analyseraster. In: Hannelore Bublitz/Andrea D. Bührmann/Christiane Hanke u.a. (Hrsg). Das Wuchern der Diskurse. Perspektiven der Diskursanalyse Foucaults, Frankfurt a.M./New York, Campus Vlg., p. 80
12. cf. Foucault, Michel 1991. Überwachen und Strafen – Die Geburt des Gefängnisses. Frankfurt a.M., Suhrkamp
13. Engelmann, Jan (Hrsg.) (1999). Foucault – Botschaften der Macht. Stuttgart, Deutsche Verlags-Anstalt, p. 215
14. cf. Foucault, Michel (1991a). Discipline And Punish – The Birth of the Prison. New York, Vintage Books, p. 198
15. ibid, p. 199
16. Foucault 1991, p. 256
17. Bentham, Jeremy (1791). Panopticon. In: Works Bd. IV. London. zit. In Foucault 1991, p. 258
18. Foucault (1991), pp. 258 – 259
19. ibid, pp. 260 – 265
20. Dauk, Elke (1989). Denken als Ethos und Methode – Foucault lesen. Berlin, Reimer, p. 127
21. Foucault (1991), p. 265.
22. Merquior, José Guilherme (1991). Foucault. London, Fontana Press, p. 92
23. Foucault 1991, p. 272
24. Foucault, Michel (1988). Für eine Politik der politischen Vernunft. In: Lettre International. Sommer 1988, p. 66
25. Marti, Urs (1988). Michel Foucault. München, Ch. Beck, p. 93
26. ibid, p. 93
27. Foucault 1991, p. 286

28. Lauenburg, Joachim (1991). Michel Foucault. In: Philosophie der Gegenwart in Einzeldarstellungen – Von Adorno bis v. Wright. Julia Nida-Rümelin (Hrsg.). Stuttgart, Kröner Vlg. 1991, p. 161

29. cf. prospect (2020). Future of Work: Employers' collection and use ofworker data. Briefing of survey results: link 20.07.2020: https://d28j9ucj9uj44t.cloudfro nt.net/uploads/2020/02/future-of-work-employers-collection-use-worker-data.pd f

30. Ponce Del Castillo, Aida (2020). Digitale Kontrolle von Beschäftigten. COVID-19 verschärft die Überwachung am Arbeitsplatz. link 07.20.2020: https: //netzpolitik.org/2020/covid-19-verschaerft-die-ueberwachung-am-arbeitsplatz/

31. ibid

32. Duschlbauer, Thomas (1998). Inofwar – Information.Macht.Krieg. blickpunkte III/1998, p. 24

33. Duschlbauer 1998, p. 24

34. Duschlbauer, Thomas (1994). Die Metamophose der Kommunikation – Vom Panopticum ins Cyberspace. Wien, Dissertation an der Universität Wien, p. 22

35. Foucaul, Michel (1976). Mikrophysik der Macht. Berlin, Merve, p. 118

36. Visker, Rudi (1991). Michel Foucault – Genealogie als Kritik. München, Fink, p. 83

37. Duschlbauer, Thomas (2001). Medien und Kultur im Zeitalter der X-Kommu-nikation. Wien, Braumüller, p. 33

38. Dauk, p. 131 – 132

39. Marti, p. 92

40. Karhama, Perti (1990). Lebensphilosophie, Moderne und Postmoderne. In: Moderne – Nietzsche – Postmoderne. Manfred Buhr (Hrsg.). Berlin, Akademie Vlg. 1990, p. 116

41. Foucault 1976, p. 109

42. Merquior, p. 110

43. Duschlbauer 1998, p. 25

44. Deleuz, Gilles & Foucault, Michel (1977). Der Faden ist gerissen. Berlin, Merve, pp. 93 – 94

45. cf. Bergmann, Frithjof & Friedland, Stella (2007). Neue Arbeit kompakt. Vision einer bestimmten Gesellschaft. Freiamt im Schwarzwald, Arbor Verlag

46. cf. Bergmann, Frithjof (2005). Die Freiheit leben. Freiamt im Schwarzwald, Arbor Verlag

47. Poppenborg, Mark (2017). 8 Dinge, die jeder über New Work wissen sollte. link 07.20.2020: https://intrinsify.de/8-dinge-die-jeder-ueber-new-work-wissen-s ollte/

48. Bilton, Chris (2007). Management and creativity: From creative industries to creative management. Oxford, Blackwell Publishing, pp. 108 – 111

49. ibid, p. 111

From phenomena to methodology

The tendency of posthocratic organisations towards radical constructivism is not only accompanied by a description of a current phenomenon, but also by ways to develop a methodology. For the work in an organisation, this would mean that it is not so much a matter of describing a reality, but rather of producing or simulating it (1), for example in the form of an intervention or staging. The results of these activities function like the original performativa in John Austin's theory of speech acts: they not only represent reality, but literally produce it in interaction processes or change it by triggering or directing actions.

Performative inquiry: A scenario test on the acceptance of new technologies with the dummy of a chatbot for the residents of a retirement home, whereby the nursing staff were involved in the hidden theatre of a "scientific" experiment.

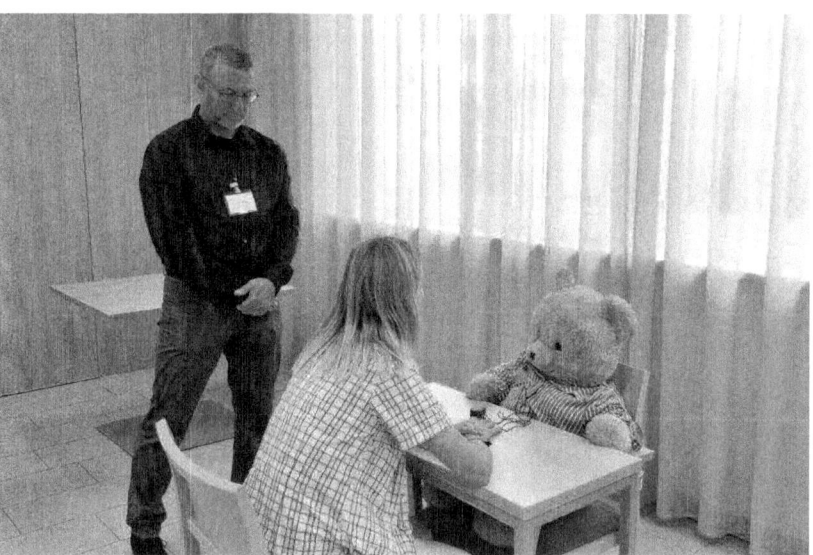

Image 2: Thomas Duschlbauer

Performative actions as reality-constituting acts are thus self-referential in so far as they mean exactly what they do. Institutional and social conditions determine how they proceed, as does the specific performance situation. Where corporate cultures "occur" in this sense, where they meet, interact and transform themselves – for example in the context of an acquisition – performativity becomes the sign of their constitution, organization, and reflection. Performative processes are not merely a possible methodology for gaining knowledge – they are in themselves immediate transformation processes that are in principle not completely plannable, controllable, or readily available. They open up spaces for play and freedom; and the unplanned, unpredictable, always appears in them – and that has a significant influence on the process of transformation. Intention and contingency, planning and emergence, are inseparably linked in them. Because of this immediacy, it seems regrettable that such performative learning processes have rarely been empirically investigated in connection with the corresponding action practices within the organization. After all, this method is also useful as a transformative instrument in organizations – and it is effective right from the time when its application is initiated.

In this context, however, the possibilities of empiricism are limited since such performative acts have an artistic and thus more or less genuine character. Besides, they are always dependent on certain situations in particular corporate cultures. Hence, such approaches have emerged against the background of an art practice that seeks to establish itself alongside the sciences as artistic research. It also aims at attaining the status of practice-led research within empirical social research and even claims independent status.

It will therefore not be easy to make predictions about such processes, let alone propose specific interventions that are purely based on empiricism. In this respect, empiricism will rather remain at the level of description. Furthermore, it will probably be difficult to say anything fundamental about the effects of the use of performativity; because the fact that an organization makes use of this kind of methodology is in and of itself an indication of an open corporate culture. The empirical view would therefore probably focus on those companies that have already taken a significant step towards change: stimulating curiosity.

In the organisation, such a methodology would probably achieve something similar to what Slavoj Žižek calls a "monstrous act". It is about anticipating the effects of something that is still hidden by showing its possible symptoms and thus helping us to understand its cause. This is because these causal elements are usually only constituted later through symbolisation. According to Jacques Lacan, truth also arises from misrecognition, which we can consciously provoke with this technique because mistakes, misunderstandings or misconceptions keep us from seeing that there never was something like an original or unbiased reality. For example, such a method can be applied to develop scenarios for the future or to assess the possible consequences of the use of new technologies better (2).

One of the special components of performativity in teamwork extends from Jacques Derrida's distinct handling of time crafted into the term "différance". This neologism describes a structuring principle that assumes that a term is not possible based on its nature, but only through its positive and negative references to other terms (3). The meaning of the language is subject to changes over time, which is why it cannot be clearly assigned:

> *Différance, a Derridian performative in itself, clarifies past and present where the future hinges on performatives in the present. (This is only one aspect of différance used here to illustrate a point.) The example Jacques Derrida uses is "Je t'aime" (translated as "I love you"), which may not be a statement of fact, a constative utterance, but rather a performative with a difference/différance that establishes a condition of a new person, one in love with another person. Time is somewhat suspended in developing a future as the truth or falsehood of the statement cannot be known without endorsement of a return performative ... (4)*

If we use performance as expressions of team performativity, the theatre could be able to offer us a place for co-created knowledge about processes and functions of team experiences. Through artful enquiry, a significant space becomes available where, *"something new is possible – where disruption occurs and the new begins"* (5). The transformation of points of struggle into points of insight is a co-experienced moment of shared epistemology. Performative inquiry (6) can be described as the exploration of a topic or issue through performance (7) and it *"opens spaces of intertextual play within which social responsibility and individual and communal response may be investigated (8), ... provides a momentary entrance into 'other' worlds embodied in play and reflection"*, and *"is a research methodology that recognizes and honours the absences, journey-landscapes, and space-moments of learning ... "* (9).

One kind of this performative examination would be forum theatre as a form of interactive theatre that goes back to Augusto Boal. He believed that everyone can be an artist and an actor. It was important to him to stage and publicise social structures. This visualisation and alienation provide essential impulses for change, i.e. perceiving, finding, trying out and further developing options for action on an individual level as well as on the level of small groups or communities. (10)

Accordingly, forum theatre assumes that everyone has something to say and it opens up spaces for people to explore their problems and social conflicts. With the participation of the audience, alternatives for action in and solutions to conflict-prone situations are developed on stage. This creates a wide range of effective options for action and solutions. In this context, forms of invisible theatre are also suitable, whose interventions can be moved from the public sphere to the premises of a company.

Invisible or "hidden" theatre developed by communist theatre groups in the 1920s and 1930s and rediscovered by Boal in the 1960s is more likely to lead to a feeling of uncertainty and provocation within an organisation than the more pedagogical project of a forum theatre. This is mainly due to the fact that the audience or the employees do not know that they are spectators and that theatre is being performed in front of their eyes. They initially experience the event as a normal everyday situation that is alienated or exaggerated and can escalate or suddenly change direction. In addition, invisible theatre also demands more improvisation skills from the actors, especially since the course of such an intervention or the reactions of the employees are unpredictable.

A contrast to hidden theatre with its intended insecurity could be in the joint development of rituals. Once these are integrated into the everyday life of an organisation, they provide a hold even in difficult situations and promote mutual trust. According to sociologist Andreas Reckwitz, social practice manifests itself in the routined processes of everyday life; it is not to be sought in 'inter-subjectivity' and not in 'norm guidance', not even in 'communication', but rather in the collectivity of behaviour held together by specific 'practical skills' (11). Accordingly, empirical interest today is directed not only at internal or external reasons – to motivations, explanations, must and should – but also to actual doing, to everyday practices and the implicit knowledge embodied therein. Because even those who have no explicit knowledge of what they are doing, because it is unconscious or cannot be put into words (and therefore they cannot talk about it in interviews, for example), still give information about it – through action.

Therefore, through performativity or the play with uncertainty and constant changeability, we can achieve a more confident handling of our world and ultimately our own identity in relation to it. Wulf and Zirfas also emphasize that in the execution of performative acts there is always the possibility of suspending the norms and rules in the execution itself, ironizing them, recoding them, questioning their unquestionability (12).

113

In general, it should be emphasised that not only theatre methods, but also dance, elements of performance and experimental formats can be used. In addition to artistic and aesthetic processes, everyday practices can also become the focus of performative research. It is about specific, practical engagement, the prudent treatment of social practices, of materials, the body, space, and even of ideas. Moreover, it is also important that these projects are developed in a participatory manner and that the participants are both viewers and actors.

References:
1. Bilton, Chris (2007). Management and creativity: From creative industries to creative management. Oxford, Blackwell Publishing, pp. 108 – 111
2. cf. Žižek, Slavoj (1999). The Sublime Object of Ideology, Ernesto Laclau and Chantal Mouffe, London, New York, Verso, pp. 57 – 59
3. cf. Derrida, Jacques (2015). Die Différance. In: Peter Engelmann (Hrsg.). Postmoderne und Dekonstruktion. Stuttgart, Reclam, pp. 80 – 82
4. Sommerfeldt, Susan C., Caine, Vera & Molzahn, Anita (2014). Considering Performativity as Methodology and Phenomena. Forum Qualitative Sozialforschung / Forum: Qualitative Social Research, 15(2), Art. 11, link 07.20.2020: http://nbn-resolving.de/urn:nbn:de:0114-fqs1402112
5. Bergum, Vangie & Godkin, Dianne (2008). Nursing research and the transformative value of art. Handbook of the Arts in Qualitative Research, p. 604
6. cf. Fels, Lynn. & McGivern, Lynne. (2002). Intertextual Play through Performative Inquiry: Intercultural Recognitions. Body and Language: Intercultural Learning Through Drama. Gerd Brauer (ed.). Atlanta, Emory University, Greenwood Academic Press
7. ibid, p. 27
8. ibid, p. 30
9. ibid, p. 32
10. Duschlbauer, Thomas & Freisleben-Teutscher, Christian F. (2017) Guerilla: Exploration, Improvisation und Kommunikation. Baden-Baden, Nomos, pp. 86 – 87
11. Reckwitz, Andreas (2003). Grundelemente einer Theorie sozialer Praktiken: Eine sozialtheoretische Perspektive. In: Zeitschrift für Soziologie, Jg. 32, H. 4, 2003, p. 289
12. Wulf, Christoph & Zirfas, Jörg (2007). Performative Pädagogik und performative Bildungstheorien. In: Dies.: Pädagogik des Performativen. Theorien. Methoden, Perspektiven. Weinheim/Basel, Beltz, p. 17

Bibliography

Adorno, Theodor W. (1973). Negative Dialectics. Trans. E.B. Ashton, London, Routledge & Kegan

Agre, P.E.(2003). Peer-to-Peer and the Promise of Internet Equality.Communications of the ACM,46(2), pp. 39 – 42

Allert, Heidrun & Richter, Christoph (2009). Design as Open-Ended Inquiry. In: V. Hornung-Prähauser, M. Luckmann and D. Wieden-Bischof (Ed.). Creativity and Innovation Competencies on the Web. 5th Interdisciplinary EduMedia Conference, Salzburg, Austria, May 4-5, 2008. Salzburg Research, pp. 206 – 221

Augustinus, Aurelius (2002). On the Trinity. Cambridge, Cambridge University Press, trin. 11,2,3

Austin, John Longshaw (1972). Zur Theorie der Sprechakte (How to do things with Words). Deutsche Bearbeitung von Eike von Savigny. Stuttgart, Reclam

Austin, John. Longshaw. (1986). Performative Äußerungen. In: Ders. Gesammelte philosophische Aufsätze. Stuttgart, Reclam

Baier, Karl (2013). Somnabulismus als Medium der Vergesellschaftung. Mesmerisch beeinflusste Auffassungen des Sozialen vom 18. zum späten 19. Jahrhundert. In: Nacim Ghanbari & Marcus Hahn (Hrsg.). Reinigungsarbeit. transcript, Zeitschrift für Kulturwissenschaften, Heft 1/2013, pp. 65 – 80

Barthes, Roland (1977). Writing Degree Zero. Selected and trans. Annette Leavers & Colin Smith,. New York, Hill and Wang

Bauer, Robert (2007). Organizations as Orientation Systems – Some Remarks on the Aesthetic Dimension of Organisational Design. Michael Shamiyeh, (Ed.). In Organizing for Change. Integrating architectural thinking into other fields. Basel, Birkhäuser, pp. 34 – 49

Bauer, Thomas (2018). Die Vereindeutigung der Welt. Über den RRoberVerlust an Mehrdeutigkeit und Vielfalt. Stuttgart, Reclam

Bentham, Jeremy (1791). Panopticon. In: Works Bd. IV. London. zit. In Foucault 1991

Bergmann, Frithjof (2005). Die Freiheit leben. Freiamt im Schwarzwald, Arbor Verlag

Bergmann, Frithjof & Friedland, Stella (2007). Neue Arbeit kompakt. Vision einer bestimmten Gesellschaft. Freiamt im Schwarzwald, Arbor Verlag

Bergmann, Frithjof (2019). New Work New Culture, Work We Want And A Culture That Strengthens Us. Winchester, Washington, John Hunt Publishing, zero books

Bergum, Vangie & Godkin, Dianne (2008). Nursing research and the transformative value of art. Handbook of the Arts in Qualitative Research, pp. 603 – 612

Bilton, Chris (2007). Management and creativity: From creative industries to creative management. Oxford, Blackwell Publishing

Blumenthal, David R. 1980: Understanding Jewish Mysticism: In History, Religion, and Spiritual Democracy: Essays in Honor of Joseph L. Blau. Ed. M. Wohlgelernter, New York, Columbia University Press, pp. 114 – 129

Boehler, Arno (2012). Deleuze in Spinoza – Spinoza in Deleuze. In: Violetta L. Waibel (Ed.): Affektenlehre und amor Dei intellectualis. Die Rezeption Spinozas im Deutschen Idealismus. In der Frühromantik und in der Gegenwart. Hamburg, Meiner Verlag, pp. 167 – 189

Borch, Christian (2009). Schaum-Organisationen: Über das Management von Atmosphären. In: Die Vermessung des Ungeheuren. Die Philosophie nach Peter Sloterdijk. Wilhelm Funk Verlag

Borch, Christian & Stäheli, Urs (Hrsg.) (2009). Einleitung. Soziologie der Nachahmung und des Begehrens: Materialien zu Gabriel Tarde. Frankfurt a.M., Suhrkamp

Bouveresse, Jacques (1995). Wittgenstein reads Freud, The myth of the unconscious. Princeton, Princeton University Press

Buchholz, Kai (2000). Sémantique formelle et ressemblances de famille. In: Logique et Analyse

Büchner, Stefanie; Kühl, Stefan & Muster Judith (2017). Ironie der Digitalisierung. Weswegen Steuerungsphantasien zu kurz greifen. Working Paper 13/2017, Universität Bielefeld

Burrell, Gibson & Morgan, Gareth (1979). Sociological Paradigms and Organisational Analysis. London/ Exeter, NH. Heinemann

Butler, Judith (1993). Bodies that Matter: On the discursive limits of „sex„. New York, London: Routledge

Canavero, Sergio (2017). Medicus magnus: Die Revolution der Medizin und wie wir sie für uns nützen. Wien, edition a

Chia, Robert (2003). Organization Theory as a Postmodern Science. Oxford, The Oxford Handbook of Organization Theory

Christensen, Clayton (1997). The Innovator's Dilemma: When New Technologies Cause Great Firms to Fail. Boston, Harvard Business Press

Citton, Yves (2010). « Le style comme filtre. Économie de l'attention et goûts philosophiques », Critique n° 752-753 janvier 2010, n° double spécial « Du style ! » pp. 24 – 35

Czarniawska, Barbara (2009). Gabriel Tarde and Organization Theory. In: Paul Adler (ed.). The Oxford Handbook of Sociology and Organization Studies: Classical Foundations. Oxford, Oxford University Press

Czarniawska, Barbara (2017). Organizational Change – Fashions. Institutions, and Translations. In: The Palgrave Handbook of Organizational Change Thinkers. Cham Palgrave Macmillan, pp. 361 – 377

Dauk, Elke (1989). Denken als Ethos und Methode – Foucault lesen. Berlin, Reimer

Deleuze, Gilles, Guattari Félix. (1974). Anti-Ödipus: Kapitalismus und Schizophrenie I. Frankfurt a.m, Suhrkamp

Deleuze, Gilles & Foucault, Michel (1977). Der Faden ist gerissen. Berlin, Merve

Deleuze, Gilles (1983). Cours sur le cinéma 1981-1985, disponibles en mp3 et en transcriptions sur le site « La voix de Gilles Deleuze en ligne » Vincennes, link: 07.20.2020 http://www.univ-paris8.fr/deleuze/

Deleuze, Gilles (1988). In: Abécédaire – Gilles Deleuze von A bis Z. Regie: Pierre-André Boutang Hrsg: V. Bertoncini, M. Weinmann, link (07.20.2020): https://absolutmedien.de/film/957/Ab%C3%A9c%C3%A9daire+%E2%80%93+Gilles+Deleuze+von+A+bis+Z

Deleuze, Gille & Guatarri Felix (1991). Was ist Philosophie? Frankfurt a. M., Suhrkamp

Deleuze, Gilles (1992). Expressionism in Philosophy: Spinoza. New York: Zone Books.

Deleuze, Gilles, Guattari Félix (1992). Tausend Plateaus. Kapitalismus und Schizophrenie II. Berlin, Merve Verlag

Deleuze, Gille & Guatarri Felix (1994). What is philosophy? New York, Columbia Press

Derrida, Jacques (1993). Die Différance. In: Postmoderne und Dekonstruktion. Stuttgart, Reclam

Derrida, Jacques (2001). „Signatur Ereignis Kontext„. In: Limited Inc. Hrsg. von Peter Engelmann. Wien, Passagen

Derrida, Jacques (2015). Die Différance. In: Peter Engelmann (Hrsg.). Postmoderne und Dekonstruktion. Stuttgart, Reclam

Descartes, René (2001). Bericht über die Methode. Ditzingen: Stuttgart, Reclam

Dieckmann, Friedrich (2005). Imperative des erfüllten Augenblicks. In: Interpretationen, Gedichte von Johann Wolfgang von Goethe. Bernd Witte (Hrsg.), Stuttgart, Reclam, p. 289

Duschlbauer, Thomas (1994). Die Metamophose der Kommunikation – Vom Panopticum ins Cyberspace. Wien, Dissertation an der Universität Wien

Duschlbauer, Thomas (1998). Inofwar – Information.Macht.Krieg. blickpunkte III/ 1998, pp. 14 – 16

Duschlbauer, Thomas (2001). Medien und Kultur im Zeitalter der X-Kommunikation. Wien, Braumüller

Duschlbauer, Thomas, Lanz, Walter & Hattmannsdorfer, Armin. (2013). Innovationsguerilla. St. Gallen/Zürich, Midas Management

Duschlbauer, Thomas & Freisleben-Teutscher, Christian F. (2017) Guerilla: Exploration, Improvisation und Kommunikation. Baden-Baden, Nomos

Duschlbauer, Thomas (2019). Umdenken ist zu wenig. Graz, Wirtschaftsnachrichten Digitalreport, pp. 9 – 11

Elon Musk: Tesla-Autos sind bis zu 200.000 Dollar wert. In: Futurezone 07.18.2019, link (07.20.2020) https://futurezone.at/produkte/elon-musk-tesla-autos-sind-bis-zu-200000-dollar-wert/400555463

Engelmann, Jan (Hrsg.) (1999). Foucault – Botschaften der Macht. Stuttgart, Deutsche Verlags-Anstalt

Erika Fischer-Lichte. Magisterarbeit, Friedrich-Alexander-Universität Erlangen-Nürnberg

Fels, Lynn. & McGivern, Lynne. (2002). Intertextual Play through Performative Inquiry: Intercultural Recognitions. Body and Language: Intercultural Learning Through Drama. Gerd Brauer (ed.). Atlanta, Emory University, Greenwood Academic Press

Fleck, Ludwik (1980). Entstehung und Entwicklung einer wissenschaftlichen Tatsache: Eine Einführung in die Lehre vom Denkstil und Denkkollektiv. Frankfurt a.m., Suhrkamp

Foucault, Michel (1974). Vorrede zur Überschreitung. In: Von der Subversion des Wissens. Hg. u. übers. v. Walter Seitter. München

Foucaul, Michel (1976). Mikrophysik der Macht. Berlin, Merve

Foucault, Michel (1978). Dispositive der Macht. Über Sexualität, Wissen und Wahrheit. Berlin, Merve

Foucault, Michel (1986). Der Gebrauch der Lüste. Sexualität und Wahrheit 2. Band. Frankfurt a.M., Suhrkamp, Foucault, Michel (1988). Für eine Politik der politischen Vernunft. In: Lettre International. Sommer 1988

Foucault, Michel (1991a). Discipline And Punish – The Birth of the Prison. New York, Vintage Books

Foucault, Michel 1991. Überwachen und Strafen – Die Geburt des Gefängnisses. Frankfurt a.M., Suhrkamp

Francis, Davies (2015). Trump on President Bush and 9/11: 'The World Trade Center Came Down During His Reign'. link (07.20.2020): https://foreignpolicy.com/2015/10/16/trump-on-president-bush-and-911-the-world-trade-center-came-down-during-his-reign/

Frank, Manfred (1989). Einführung in die frühromantische Ästhetik, lectures. Frankfurt a. M., Suhrkamp

Frank, Manfred (1989a). Wittgensteins Gang in die Dichtung. In: Manfred Frank & Gianfranco Soldati, (Ed.), Wittgenstein. Literat und Philosoph. Pfullingen, Neske

Freud, Sigmund (1974). Das Unbehagen in der Kultur. In: Sigmund Freud: Studienausgabe, Bd. 9. Frankfurt a. M., S. Fischer

Fukuyama, Francis (1992). The End of History and the Last Man. New York, Free Press

Fukuyama, Francis (2004) Transhumanism: The World's Most Dangerous Idea. In: Foreign Policy 144

Funcke, Bettina (2005). Against Gravity. Bettina Funcke in conversation with Peter Sloterdijk. Link (07.20.2020) http://dev.autonomedia.org/node/4584

Garver, Newton & Lee, Seung-Chong (1994). Derrida and Wittgenstein. Philadelphia, Temple University Press

Gebske, Jennifer (2009). Performativität zwischen Zitation und Ereignis. Vergleich der Performativitätsbegriffe von Judith Butler und Tarde

Gehlen, Arnold (2016). Der Mensch. Seine Natur und seine Stellung in der Welt. Frankfurt a. M., Klostermann

Gladwell, Malcolm (2005). Blink. The Power of Thinking without Thinking. Boston, Back Bay Books

Glasersfeld, Ernst von (2002). Abschied von der Objektivität. In: Krieg, Peter & Watzlawick Paul (Hrsg.). Das Auge des Betrachters. Beiträge zum Konstruktivismus. Heidelberg, Carl-Auer-Systeme Verlag

Goethe, Johann Wolfgang von (1829). link (07.20.2020): https://www.poemhunter.com/poem/a-legacy-4/

Goethe, Johann Wolfgang von. (1812). Prooemion. link (07.20.2020): https://oll.libertyfund.org/titles/goethe-goethes-works-vol-1-poems?q=Prooemion#lf0841-01_head_432

Goethe, Johann Wolfgang von (1981). Goethes Werke. Erich Trunz (Hrsg.), Bd. I, Gedichte und Epen, München, Ch. Beck

Günzel, Stephan (1998): Immanenz. Zum Philosophiebegriff von Gilles Deleuze, Essen

Habermas, Jürgen (1981). Theorie des kommunikativen Handelns. (Bd. 1: Handlungsrationalität und gesellschaftliche Rationalisierung, Bd. 2: Zur Kritik der funktionalistischen Vernunft), Frankfurt a.M., Suhrkamp

Hansemann, David (1899). Ueber das Gehirn von Hermann von Helmholtz. Leipzig, Zeitschrift für Psychologie und Physiologie der Sinnesorgane, Band 20

Harari, Yuval Noah (2014). Sapiens: A Brief History of Humankind. London, Harvill Secker

Hargadon, Andrew B. & Yellowlees, Douglas (2001). When Innovations Meet Institutions: Edison and the Design of the Electric Light. In: Administrative Science Quarterly, September 2001, pp. 476 – 501

Hegele-Raih, Cornelia (2006). Was ist … Isomorphismus? In: Harvard Business Manager, link (07.20.2020): https://www.manager-magazin.de/harvard/print/hm/d-47632104.html

Heintz,Bettina(2016). Welterzeugung durch Zahlen. Modelle politischer Differenzierung in internationalen Statistiken. 1948 – 2010. Soziale Systeme, 18 (1 – 2), pp. 7 – 39

Heller, Erich (1988). The importance of Nietzsche: ten essays. Chicago/London, University of Chicago Press

Hirseland, Andreas & Schneider, Werner (2008). Biopolitik und Technologien des Selbst: zur Subjektivierung von Macht und Herrschaft. In: K.-S. Rehberg (Hrsg.). Die Natur der Gesellschaft: Verhandlungen des 33. Kongresses der Deutschen Gesellschaft für Soziologie in Kassel 2006. Teilbd. 1 u. 2, Frankfurt a. M., Campus Verl., pp. 5640 – 5648

Ignatius, Adi (2015). The Disruption Conversation. In: Harvard Business Review, December 2015 Issue, p. 14

Isabelle Stengers (2009). Au temps des catastrophes. Résister à la barbarie qui vient. Paris, La Découverte/Les empêcheurs de penser en rond

Jackson, Shannon (2011). Social Worlds. Performing Art, Supporting Publics. London/New York: Routledge

Jünger, Ernst (1979). Strahlungen I. In: Sämtliche Werke, Band 2. Tagebücher II, Stuttgart, Klett-Cotta Verlag

Kant, Immanuel (1998) Kritik der reinen Vernunft. Hamburg, Meiner Verlag

Karhama, Perti (1990). Lebensphilosophie, Moderne und Postmoderne. In: Moderne – Nietzsche – Postmoderne. Manfred Buhr (Hrsg.). Berlin, Akademie Vlg. 1990

Kerres, Michael & Witt, Caudia de (2004). Pragmatismus als theoretische Grundlage zur Konzeption von eLearning. In: D. Treichel & H.O.

Kertschner, Jens (2003). Wittgenstein- Austin- Derrida. „Performativität" in der sprachphilosophischen Diskussion. In: Jens Kertscher & Dieter Mersch (Hg.): Performativität und Praxis. München, Wilhelm Fink Vlg.

Kinnunen, Jussi (1996). Gabriel Tarde as a founding father of innovation diffusion research. Acta Sociologica, Vol. 39, pp. 431 - 442

Lanham, Richard A. (2006). The Economics of Attention. Style and Substance in the Age of Information. Chicago, University of Chicago Press

Latour, Bruno (2007). L'Espoir de Pandore. Pour une version réaliste de l'activité scientifique. Paris, La Découverte

Latour, Bruno (2015). Some experiments in art and politics. In: Aranda J, Wood BK, Vidokle A (eds.) The Internet does not exist – e-flux Journal, Berlin, Sternberg Press

Lauenburg, Joachim (1991). Michel Foucault. In: Philosophie der Gegenwart in Einzeldarstellungen – Von Adorno bis v. Wright. Julia Nida-Rümelin (Hrsg.). Stuttgart, Kröner Vlg. 1991

Lemke, Thomas (2013). Gesellschaftskörper und Organismuskonzepte: Überlegungen zur Bedeutung von Metaphern in der soziologischen Theo-rie. In: Die Natur in der Soziologie. Gesellschaftliche Voraussetzungen und Folgen biotechnologischen Wissens. Frankfurt a.M, Campus-Verlag

Lepore, Jill (2014). The Disruption Machine. What the gospel of innovation gets wrong. In: The New Yorker, June 16, 2014. link (07.20.2020) https://www.newyorker.com/magazine/2014/06/23/the-disruption-machine

Linstead, Stephen (2004). Organisation Theory and Postmodern Thought. New York, Sage

Lohweide, Bernward (2000). Fichte und Novalis. Amsterdam, Editions Rodopi B.V.

Luchte, James (2016). Mortal Thought. London, Bloomsbury

Lüdemann, Susanne (2009). Die imaginäre Gesellschaft. Gabriel Tardes anti-naturalistische Soziologie der Nachahmung. In: Christian Borch & Urs Stäheli (Hrsg.). Soziologie der Nachahmung und des Begehrens – Materialien zu Gabriel Tarde. Frankfurt a.M., Suhrkamp

Luhmann, Niklas (1997). Die Gesellschaft der Gesellschaft. Frankfurt a.M., Suhrkamp

Lyotard, Jean-François (1979). Apathie der Theorie. Berlin, Merve

Lyotard, Jean-François (1984). The Postmodern Condition: A Report on Knowledge. Minneapolis, University of Minnesota Press

Marsden, Paul (2000). Forefathers of Memetics: Gabriel Tarde and the Laws of Imitation. Journal of Mimetics-Evolutionary Models of Information Transmission, Vol. 4, n°1, pp. 61 – 66

Marti, Urs (1988). Michel Foucault. München, Ch. Beck

Marx, Karl & Engels, Frederick (1848). Manifesto of the Communist Party. London

McLuhan, Marshall (1964). Understanding Media. London, Routledge & Keg

Merquior, José Guilherme (1991). Foucault. London, Fontana Press

Mersch, Dietmar (2002). Was sich zeigt. Materialität, Präsenz, Ereignis. München, Wilhelm Fink Verlag

Meyer (Hrsg.): Handlungsorientiertes Lernen und eLearning. Grundlagen und Beispiele. München, Oldenbourg Verlag (uncorrected draft)

Müller, Gin (2015). Possen des Performativen. Wien, Transversal

Neumann, John (2014). Die Rechenmaschine und das Gehirn. München, De Gruyter

Neuscheler, Tillmann & Peitsmeier, Henning (2020). Der Fall Wirecard: Mit Korpsgeist und Treueschwüren. In FAZ 22.07.2020. link: 07.24.2020: https://www.faz.net/aktuell/wirtschaft/wirecard-mit-korpsgeist-und-treueschwueren-16872208.html

Ohler, Matthias (1990). Sprachphilosophie oder Sprachwissenschaft? In: Fritz Wallner & Arne Haselbach (Ed.). Wittgensteins Einfluß auf die Kultur der Gegenwart. Philosophica 9, Wien, Wilhelm Braumüller

Ponce Del Castillo, Aida (2020). Digitale Kontrolle von Beschäftigten. COVID-19 verschärft die Überwachung am Arbeitsplatz. link 07.20.2020: https://netzpolitik.org/2020/covid-19-verschaerft-die-ueberwachung-am-arbeitsplatz/

Poppenborg, Mark (2017). 8 Dinge, die jeder über New Work wissen sollte. link 07.20.2020: https://intrinsify.de/8-dinge-die-jeder-ueber-new-work-wissen-sollte/

Power, Michael (1990). Modernism, postmodernism, management and organization. In: J. Hassard & D. Pym (Hrsg.), The theory and philosophy of organizations. Critical issues and new perspectives (Social analysis) London: Routledge, pp. 109 – 124

prospect (2020). Future of Work: Employers' collection and use ofworker data. Briefing of survey results: link 20.07.2020: https://d28j9ucj9uj44t.cloudfront.net/uploads/2020/02/future-of-work-employers-collection-use-worker-data.pdf

Reckwitz, Andreas (2003). Grundelemente einer Theorie sozialer Praktiken: Eine sozialtheoretische Perspektive. In: Zeitschrift für Soziologie, Jg. 32, H. 4, 2003, pp. 282 – 301

Reckwitz, Andreas (2004). Die Reproduktion und die Subversion sozialer Praktiken. Zugleich ein Kommentar zu Pierre Bourdieu und Judith Butler. In: Karl H. Hörning (Hrsg.): Doing Culture. Zum Begriff der Praxis in der gegenwärtigen soziologischen Theorie, Bielefeld

Reijers, Wessel & Coeckelbergh, Mark (2018). The Blockchain as a Narrative Technology: Investigating the Social Ontology and Normative Configurations of Cryptocurrencies. Philos. Technol. 31, pp. 103 – 130

Revell, Timothy (2018). How to stop artificial intelligence being so racist and sexist. In: newscientist.com, link (07.20.2020) https://www.newscientist.com/article /2173472-how-to-stop-artificial-intelligence-being-so-racist-and-sexist/#ixzz6SrqE GVjr

Rogers, Everet M. (1995). Diffusion of innovation. New York, The Free Press

Sadin, Éric (7. Juni 2017). Das geht zu weit! In: Die Zeit, Nr. 24

Sandelands, Lloyd & Drazin, Robert (1989). On the Language of Organization Theory. Organization Studies, Vol. 10, pp. 457 – 477

Saussure, Ferdinand de (1997). Linguistik und Semiologie. Notizen aus dem Nachlaß. Texte, Briefe und Dokumente, gesammelt, übersetzt und eingeleitet v. Johannes Fehr, Frankfurt/M., Suhrkamp

Schlingensief, Christoph (2006). Ausländer Raus! DVD documentation, producer Paul Poet, Wien, Hoanzl

Schlippe, Arist von & Schweitzer, J. (2016). Lehrbuch der systemischen Therapie und Beratung I und II. Göttingen, Vandenhoeck & Ruprecht

Schulte, Joachim (1990). Chor und Gesetz: Wittgenstein im Kontext. Frankfurt a.M., Suhrkamp

Schulz, Walter (1979). Wittgenstein: Die Negation der Philosophie. Neske, Pfullingen

Schumpeter, Joseph (1912). Theorie der wirtschaftlichen Entwicklung. Berlin, Duncker & Humblot

Seier, Andrea (1999). Kategorien der Entzifferung: Macht und Diskurs als Analyseraster. In: Hannelore Bublitz/Andrea D. Bührmann/Christiane Hanke u.a. (Hrsg). Das Wuchern der Diskurse. Perspektiven der Diskursanalyse Foucaults, Frankfurt a.M./New York, Campus Vlg.

Seitz, Tim (2017). Design Thinking und der neue Geist des Kapitalismus. Bielefeld, transcript

Shakespeare, William (1623). As you like it. London, Penguin Books

Shamiyeh, Michael (2014). Discontinuous Change and Organizational Response: Exploring the Moderating Effects of Resources and Capabilities – the Case of Kodak. Disseration at the University of St. Gallen

Shelley, Mary (2013). Frankenstein; or, The Modern Prometheus. Stuttgart, Reclam

Simon, Herbert A. (1959). Theories of decision making in economics and behavioural science. In: American Economic Review, Vol. 49, Nr. 3, pp. 253 – 283

Sloterdijk, Peter (2004). Sphären III – Schäume. Frankfurt a.M., Suhrkamp

Sommerfeldt, Susan C., Caine, Vera & Molzahn, Anita (2014). Considering Performativity as Methodology and Phenomena. Forum Qualitative Sozialforschung / Forum: Qualitative Social Research, 15(2), Art. 11, link 07.20.2020: http://nbn-re solving.de/urn:nbn:de:0114-fqs1402112

Sontag, Susan (1990). Against Interpretation, New York, Picador

Staten, Henry (1985). Wittgenstein and Derrida. Oxford, Basil Blackwell

Stern, Josef P. (1990). Literarische Aspekte der Schriften Ludwig Wittgensteins. In: Wittgenstein und. Wendelin Schmidt-Dengler, Martin Huber & Michael Hutter (Ed.), Wien, Edition S.

Steuerman, Emilia (1992). Habermas vs. Lyotard: Modernity vs. Postmodernity. In: Judging Lyotard, Benjamin, A. (Ed.), London/New York, Routledge

Tarde, Gabriel de (1903): The laws of imitation. New York, Henry Holt and Company (Orig: Les lois de l'imitation 1890)

Tarde, Gabriel de (1993). Les lois de l'imitation. Paris, Editions Kimé

Tarde, Gabriel de (2003): Die Gesetze der Nachahmung. Frankfurt a.M., Suhrkamp

Tarde, Gabriel de (2009). Monadologie und Soziologie. Frankfurt a.M., Suhrkamp

Ternes, Bernd (2016). Essay zur Technologie nach der Postmoderne mit besonderer Berücksichtigung des Satzes von Vilém Flusser: „Ich lebe so oft, wie ich durch Vernetzung an Verknotungen teilnehme". In: Kritiknetz - Zeitschrift für Kritische Theorie der Gesellschaft

Visker, Rudi (1991). Michel Foucault – Genealogie als Kritik. München, Fink

Volbers, Jörg (2017). Die offene Praxis der Sprache. Wittgensteins und Austins pragmatische Wende der Sprachphilosophie. In: Bedorf/Gerlek (Eds.): Philosophien der Praxis

Watzlawick, Paul. (2002). Einleitung. In: Krieg, Peter & Watzlawick Paul (Hrsg.). Das Auge des Betrachters. Beiträge zum Konstruktivismus. Heidelberg, Carl-Auer-Systeme Verlag

Weik, Elke (1997). Postmoderne Ansätze in der Organisationstheorie. Wiesbaden, Gabler

Weik, Karl E. (1995). Sensemaking in Organizations. New York, Sage

Weizsäcker, Carl Friedrich von (1955). Nachwort in Goethes Werke. Bd. XIII, Naturwissenschaftliche Schriften, Hamburg, Christian Wegner Vlg.

Wiesing, Lambert (1992). Pluralität durch ästhetisches Denken. In: Postmoderne oder: Das Ende des Suchens. Eggingen, Edition Isele, pp. 110 – 126

Willke, Helmut (2001). Systemisches Wissensmanagement. Stuttgart, UTB Vlg.

Wittgenstein, Ludwig (1953). Philosophical Investigations. Trans. G.E.M. Anscomb, Oxford, Basil Blackwell

Wittgenstein, Ludwig (1963). Tractatus logico-philosophicus, Frankfurt a. M., Suhrkamp

Wittgenstein, Ludwig (1964). Philosophische Bermerkungen. Frankfurt a.M., Suhrkamp

Wittgenstein, Ludwig (1988). Culture and Value. Ed. by G.H. von Wright, transl. Peter Winch, Oxford, Basil Blackwell

Wittgenstein, Ludwig (1989). Vorlesungen 1930-1935. Frankfurt a.M., Suhrkamp

Wittgenstein, Ludwig (1994). Vermischte Bemerkungen. Frankfurt a. M., Suhrkamp

Wulf, Christoph & Zirfas, Jörg (2007). Performative Pädagogik und performative Bildungstheorien. In: Dies.: Pädagogik des Performativen. Theorien. Methoden, Perspektiven. Weinheim/Basel, Beltz, pp. 7 – 12

Žižek, Slavoj (1999). The Sublime Object of Ideology, Ernesto Laclau and Chantal Mouffe, London, New York, Verso

The Author

Thomas Duschlbauer teaches at the University of Applied Sciences in St. Pölten and at the University of Applied Sciences in Hagenberg. Currently, he works for a project concerning demographic change within business organisations that is co-funded by the EU.

He has had several research stays in the USA and the UK and (co-)published books on media, culture, innovation and guerrilla. Thomas Duschlbauer does consultancy for international companies like Siemens, Primetals Technologies and voestalpine. He is also an activist in the Social Impact AG and participates in performances and interventions in public space such as hidden theatre, social sculptures, etc.

Image 3: Christof Huemer